ACKNOWLEDGEME[N]

C000221789

It can be surprising at times when y[...] [...]ge of days gone by, and for many in the [...] [...]ut its industrial past with the various [...] [...]ss shaped the towns we live in today, [...] [...] [...] [...]ew Town. The other main topic, like most parts of Scotland is the love of football. Here in this day and age many of the sizable towns in the County have their Junior football teams, nearly all of them having their moments of glory and great teams of the past, a good few winning the ultimate prize at that level the Scottish Junior Cup. But what a good few people didn't know was, that many towns in the County had teams entering the senior equivalent : the Scottish Football Association Challenge Cup. This competition brought along teams to our towns and villages such as Celtic, Rangers, Hibernian & Heart of Midlothian long before our most recent senior team Livingston appeared on the scene. This book delves into the past and gives a complete account of all Scottish Cup matches played in West Lothian. Early matches proved difficult in the way of reports when the game itself was still developing, and local papers more or less recorded the final result and little more. It wasn't until the beginning of the twentieth century and onwards when the game became firmly established that we got more in-depth reports, and this improved even more when local clubs were to be admitted to the Scottish League. As well as a complete record of all Scottish Cup matches played the book also covers the Scottish Qualifying Cup. Enjoy the adventures of your local team as well as your near neighbours. Who was the most successful? I will leave that for you to decide. I hope you enjoy reading as much as I have enjoyed writing, at times it's been a nightmare putting things together but due to the help of many others it has finally got into print, so I finish this introduction with the many names that helped make this book possible, not in any particular order I thank the advertisers, West Lothian Library staff, my wife Nicky, David Stoker, Stewart McLean, Iain MacNeil, Jo Paterson, and finally Alan Davies & Linda Davies.

MAP 0.1 WEST LOTHIAN

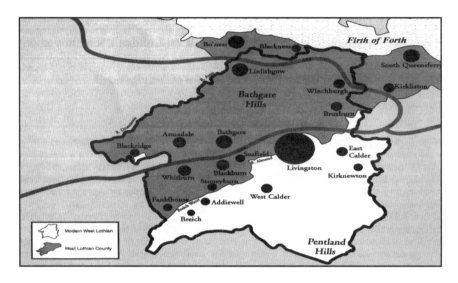

New & old West Lothian boundaries, reproduced courtesy of Stuart Borrowman

INTRODUCTION TO THE SCOTTISH CUP

The Scottish Cup is the world's oldest football trophy, first played for as far back as 1873-74 and still being played to this day. Nowadays, once the winners have been presented with the original trophy and have done their lap of honour, it is replaced with a replica trophy. Eight clubs came together to form the Scottish Football Association on the 13th March 1873, and the new organisation collected £53-12s-11d in order to institute a Challenge Cup, which included a set of medals. Sixteen teams took part in the very first competition, with Queens Park coming out worthy winners. The first couple of years were dominated by west coast sides, although by 1875-76 we saw the appearance of Edinburgh clubs. By 1881 the first clubs in this area appeared in West Calder and Addiewell, even though at that time they were just over the border in the County of Midlothian. With border changes in 1975, the above towns came under the West Lothian banner, and Bo'ness and South Queensferry left the County.

SCOTTISH CUP NOTES

Apart from the first couple of seasons up until 1890/91 season, early rounds were played on a geographical basis due to the vast amounts of teams involved in the competition. From 1891/92 till 1894/95 season, preliminary rounds were introduced, and this was followed by the Scottish Qualifying Cup in season 1895/96 where the last sixteen teams left in the competition would automatically be entered into the Scottish Cup. Clubs failing to get past the early stages of the Qualifying Cup would enter the Scottish Consolation Cup tournament, which only lasted seven seasons. There was a change in format from 2007-08 season, where the Qualifying Cup was mothballed, and this saw all the usual competitors join the Scottish Cup, along with the successful junior sides, and also clubs from the lower reaches of the Scottish League in the first round.

In this book you will come across matches which are known as "walkovers" (w/o). This practice was more common in the early years of the competition, and still happens to this day, but in a less frequent manner. If a club fails to play a particular cup tie, it is known for the team to scratch. This can be done for various reasons, i.e. money, travel, failing to produce a team etc. However, in some particular ties the reasons are mentioned in the book, but others are unknown. The way it is recorded in this book is with a "W" for the side entering the next round with an "O" for the club scratching. A club receiving a bye into the next round is self explanatory.

THE CLUBS INVOLVED

This chapter will unravel the clubs and towns involved, and hopefully give a clearer picture when reading the book. You only have to look at Broxburn, and to a lesser extent Bathgate, to realise how difficult it can be with the amount of teams that took part from West Lothian in the National competition; thankfully other towns were a little less confusing when researching.

Starting off with Broxburn; this town owes so much of its expansion to the shale oil industry. Before the discovery of large quantities of shale oil in the area, the village of Broxburn was a quiet, peaceful farming community with a population of around 2,000. By the early 1860's- practically "overnight"- the village was to change for ever, with a huge influx of men and their families arriving in their thousands, many coming over from Ireland to work in the mines and oil works.

Around the early 1880's, football was being played by local youths who started up a team by the name of Broxburn Star. Soon after the Irish youths did likewise, with a team by the name of Broxburn Harp, the latter became the backbone of the first senior side in the town **Broxburn Shamrock**. It wasn't long before Star did likewise, and also joined the senior ranks. They too changed their name to **Broxburn Thistle**.

By this time both teams were playing at the Sports Fields, but due to the fierce rivalry between these sides both clubs owned separate goalposts, which would appear to have prompted Shamrock to move on to other premises in the town. By 1885-86 season Shamrock were first to appear in the Scottish Cup, but things didn't look rosy for the Irishmen. With the local shale industry on its knees, many of their players were forced to leave the town in search of work elsewhere, and by 1888 the club had called it a day.

There had been talk of an amalgamation between the two senior sides, but due to the strong rivalry between them things never got off the ground. Thistle carried on, but changed their name to **Broxburn Football Club**. By 1889 the club moved to its new ground, Albion Park, mainly due to the atrocious state of the Sports Fields which resembled little more than a ploughed field. By 1891, Broxburn Shamrock were back on the scene securing a ground at Pyothall. The biggest challenge to date, not only for the Broxburn clubs but for the whole of the County, was the start of professionalism in Scotland in 1893. One local reporter at the time, suggested that the County should form two senior sides with Broxburn, Bo'ness and Linlithgow making up one team while West Calder, Bathgate and Armadale made up the other half. This way it would stop larger city clubs picking off all the top players. As it turned out the following season, Broxburn FC became defunct and Shamrock continued, but they were also struggling and played only a few matches. Before the end of the century there was to be no senior football in the town with Junior club Broxburn Athletic being the main attraction for the town's football supporters.

It was not until 1901-02 season that senior football emerged with the reappearance of Broxburn FC. This time the club played on the out-skirts of the town, near the Drumshoreland Railway Station. Within a couple of seasons Broxburn Shamrock were back in the fold, managing to lease a field to the west of the village at Goschen. With struggling attendances Broxburn FC moved back to the original sports fields where a proper pitch was laid out.

By season 1905-06 the town of Broxburn boasted three senior teams when **Broxburn Athletic** stepped up from the junior ranks. With the town's population at the time around 14,000 it seemed very doubtful if all three could survive, but as it turned out the 1908-09 season saw the end once again of Broxburn Shamrock, but within a season Shamrock made a surprise return. By 1914 however, the club finally called it a day. In between this time Broxburn FC and Athletic joined forces to form **Broxburn United**, and the club were relatively successful, joining the Scottish League as well as turning out few decent cup results. Due to financial problems senior football disappeared from the town, with United going Junior in 1927. This lasted barely a couple of seasons before the club ceased to exist. Senior football made a brief appearance in 1934 with **Broxburn St Johns** playing in the Edinburgh and District League, where they managed one match in the Qualifying Cup.

Broxburn United – Sports Park © Mr.Jonathan Moore – www.uphall.org

Remaining in the district of Broxburn the village of Uphall also had a couple of senior sides with Uphall Rovers and Uphall Bluebell being the forerunners, with both sides playing out of Craigview Park to the north of the village, although neither side took part in the National Trophy. It was not until 1892, a few years after the demise of these early clubs, that we saw the appearance of **Uphall Football Club** playing out of the same ground but now under the name of Crossgreen Park. This club lasted around four seasons but did take part in the "Scottish". It was not until 1907 that we saw a new club reappear but still under the same guise of Uphall FC. This time, the club were playing to the east of the village at Goschen Park. Lasting only a couple of seasons, they did however manage to fight through the early Qualifying Cup rounds to stake their place in the Scottish Cup proper.

The final trio of villages from this corner of the County was that of Winchburgh; like Broxburn and Uphall this was another village that expanded due to the shale oil industry. When local junior side Niddry Violet became defunct in 1905 the more ardent town folk who were involved with this junior side decided to follow in the footsteps of neighbouring Broxburn Athletic, and take the next step on the football

6

ladder, thus forming senior side **West Lothian Albion.** This side was formed in 1906 continuing to play at Violet's ground the Sports Fields at Niddry to the south of the village. The club lasted until 1912, due to the close proximity of Broxburn, the clubs were always playing second fiddle to their local rivals in gathering support and indeed holding on to players, these were the major factors that spelled an end to the club.

The largest town in the County around the end of the nineteenth century was that of Bathgate. Unlike Broxburn with its large shale deposits, the Bathgate area was rich in coal with several mines in the area. Along with an Iron works, the town boasted the world's first commercial oil refinery. As early as 1879, football was being played in the town where Bathgate FC played friendly matches against local sides, but little is known about this team which barely lasted a couple of years.

The first team to make an impact was **Durhamtown Rangers**. Formed in 1883, not to be fooled by the name, this club was formed by the Irish Catholics' in the area and played out of Dedethill Park to the south of the town. Within a few years the club's name was changed more in line with their nationality to **Erin Rovers,** but by 1888 however, the club merged with Bathgate Volunteers to form **Bathgate Rovers** who played at Little Boghead. Things were to change again when Bathgate Rovers merged with Bathgate Athletic, with the new club named simply **Bathgate Football Club**. The club moved into their new home, that of Mill Park, till they finally wound up in 1932. Out of all the senior teams in the area they were easily the most successful sides in National Cup competitions in the district. Finally in 2008-09 season Junior side **Bathgate Thistle** made an appearance in the Scottish Cup. The Creamery Park side gained entry by winning the Junior equivalent the previous season.

Moving a couple of miles to the west of Bathgate we find the town of Armadale. The town expanded considerably during the mid nineteenth century, mainly due to the demand for coal and ironstone which was richly available in and around the town. The first football team to appear in the town was that of **Armadale Football Club**. Formed around 1879, they played in the town's Public Park before moving up to the Mayfield area to the south. By 1889 the club moved to Volunteer Park, where the ground was shared with Junior side Armadale Volunteers; the Volunteers however moved to Heatherfield soon after. As mentioned previously,

7

professionalism caused so many problems to the County clubs. Armadale were no different with the club struggling to an end in 1894 barely a year after the SFA had legalised professionalism. Junior side **Armadale Volunteers** filled the gap, as they stepped up to the senior level and gave the town Scottish Cup football in time for the 1896-97 season. Armadale Daisy, a newly formed junior outfit, in turn filled in the gap left from the Volunteers. The Volunteers struggled at this grade however, and by 1899 the club and senior football was once again finished in the town. It was not until 1910, when a meeting was held in the towns Forsyth's Hall with a view to starting up a senior team in the town. With the help of committee members from Armadale Thistle Juniors, they created a new club once again known simply as **Armadale Football Club**. This club went on to be the most successful side from the town, as well as some great Scottish Cup runs, the club also played in the Scottish league. Owing to financial difficulties however, the club eventually went under in 1933.

Armadale F.C. Volunteer Park © West Lothian Local History Library

Moving to the North of the County on the banks of the River Forth, we find the town of Bo'ness; a once busy port, the town also had a thriving coal industry. Senior football arrived in the town in 1881 when **Bo'ness Football Club** started what was to be a long distinguished career taking the club to the end of the Second World War. Early days saw the club play out of various grounds which included Bo'ness (Grays) Football Park, Soo & Cra Park and Whitefield Park, before finally moving to Newtown Park in 1886. During that period the club were also Scottish League members,

8

spending a year in the top division in 1927-28 season. The club eventually merged with Junior side Bo'ness Cadora to form the current Junior side **Bo'ness United.** With United winning the East Super League in 2009-10 season, the club brought back Scottish Cup football to Newtown Park after a lapse of over seventy years.

The town of Linlithgow was once the hub of the County, and boasted a couple of Senior sides with Linlithgow FC appearing around the mid 1880's, followed by **Linlithgow Athletic** a couple of years later. They played out of the town's Captain's Park which was situated to the east of the present Tesco car park. The club made a few appearances in the National Competition, but never made any real impact suffering some heavy defeats along the way. It was not until the new format of the Scottish Cup was introduced in 2007, allowing Junior sides entry to the National Competition that we saw the Scottish Cup played once again in the town. Junior outfit **Linlithgow Rose** formed as far back as 1889, have entered the competition three times gaining entry after lifting the Scottish Junior Cup twice along with the league championship. The start of 2014-15 season saw "Rose" join the SFA which enables them to take part in the Scottish Cup without having to qualify through any of the Junior competitions.

A few miles east of Linlithgow you find the hamlet of Kingscavil. Surprisingly enough, this one- time oil shale village, which at its height barely peaked a population of 1000, had its own football team by the name of **Champfleurie,** sporting an unusual nickname the "Celestials", formed as a junior outfit in 1886. They spent the tail end of their short career as seniors bowing out by 1891, during that spell they did however play hosts to Heart of Midlothian in a third round tie at Champfleurie Park. The club made a brief appearance a few years later but took no part in the national trophy.

Moving further east to the town of South Queensferry the rather unusual name of **Bellstane Birds** appeared, taking their name from an area in the town. First formed in 1882 the club played their home games at Birds Park which was situated directly behind the Hawes Inn to the east of the town, the club played at both Junior and Senior levels throughout their short stop/start career.

Heading over to the far west of the County, we come across the small coal mining community of East Benhar. This small village sat to the north of Fauldhouse, and although nothing remains of the village today, at the turn of the last century it had a population of around 600/700. Little is known about the village's team **East Benhar Rangers** who made a brief appearance in the Scottish Qualifying Cup, but in all probability they would have taken their name from the Glasgow giants as they also sported an all-blue strip.

Back into the shale mining region and to the town of Addiewell, where James Young the oil pioneer set up what at the time was Britain's largest oil refinery. **Addiewell Football Club** was to be the first side in the area to take part in the Scottish Cup. Formed in 1880, the club played at the village's Cuthill Park. The club lasted only a few seasons, entering the "Scottish" twice and on each occasion were on the receiving end of Edinburgh's "big two", with a couple of heavy defeats.

A couple of miles down the road, we find another town heavily involved in the shale oil industry, that of West Calder. **West Calder Football Club** formed in 1878, this made them the first senior side in the area. Playing at Games Park, the club managed a very creditable quarter final appearance at their first attempt of the National trophy. It wasn't long however, before the club had a rival. The small mining community of Mossend, to the north east of West Calder, had their own Senior football team by the name of **Mossend Swifts**. From such a small community, this club certainly punched well above their weight, and during the latter part of the nineteenth century the club were certainly seen as one of the top sides in the area, so much so that two players managed to grace the Scotland jersey. By 1903 however, both local clubs joined forces to form **West Calder Swifts** playing at Burngrange Park, but the new club failed to find any previous form from their past identities, very seldom making any impact in the Scottish Cup. The club continued up until the First World War but this seemed to spell the end of the club.

"A late photograph of Mossend Park"

The final piece of the jigsaw takes us to the new town of Livingston. The New Town was designated on April 16th 1962 under the New Towns act 1946. Livingston Development Corporation were then given the job to manage the new town. After thirty years at the helm, and just before it would be taken over by West Lothian Council, one of LDC's final developments was to build Almondvale Stadium. This all came about when the Corporation, and Meadowbank Thistle chairman at that time Bill Hunter, struck a deal which saw senior football return to the County for the first time since the 1930's. Part of the agreement was also to see a name change to that of **Livingston Football Club,** and the club moved into their new premises in 1995. Generally the club have been fairly successful, winning the League Cup in 2004 along with the Challenge Cup in 2015. The Scottish Cup has still eluded them, although they have made two semi final appearances. A lot of success was mainly down to the club living beyond their means, this sadly like a lot of top senior sides in Scotland at this present time, has led the club into administration on a couple of occasions. The club at the moment are still trying to find their feet and for the foreseeable future Scottish Cup glory seems a long way off.

THE BIGGER PICTURE

In 1873/74 season, the first Scottish Cup competition took place; sixteen teams took part, with Queens Park eventually lifting the trophy, after defeating Clydesdale 2-0 at (Old) Hampden Park. Queens Park went on to lift the trophy the next two seasons with wins over Renton 3-0, followed by a 2-0 victory over Third Lanark after a 1-1 draw. Vale of Leven were to win the next three cups. The first in 1876/77 took three games to decide the winners, after two 1-1

11

draws. Vale eventually lifted the trophy defeating Rangers 3-2. The following year saw a 1-0 win over Third Lanark. Vale of Leven completed the treble in controversial circumstances – Rangers had refused to play a second match after a 1-1 draw, as they felt the referee disallowed a perfectly good goal and the cup was awarded to Vale of Leven. Then after another hat-trick of wins by Queens Park, the first victory came against Thornliebank 3-0. This was followed by two wins over Dumbarton, the first of which ended 3-1 after a protested first match that Queens Park also won, this brings us up to date with the entry of the West Lothian sides (see next Bigger Picture for Queens Park's third cup win).

The first season for West Lothian clubs to enter the Scottish Cup came around in 1881/82, this was the ninth season as a whole but still very much in its infancy. It's difficult to imagine how the set-up would have looked in those early days, but it would have been fairly basic, consisting of an open field, with the actual playing surface roped off where the spectators would gather round to watch. As the game progressed, changes were made and the parks for these local sides would have improved considerably, with perimeter walls and fences enclosing the grounds. The most drastic of changes were made when four of the local sides were admitted to the Scottish League, and improvements had to be made to comply with the membership rules. Looking at Bo'ness' Newtown Park to this day still gives you an idea how things would have looked back in the twenties and thirties. Early days would also have seen very little in the way of changing facilities, where quite often a local public house would be used before pavilions were built for such uses.

It was to be West Calder and Addiewell who were to take part in the competition, but very little is known about these early ties, apart from the final scores. Addiewell visited Edinburgh to take on Hibernian, and the home side recorded an easy 7-0 victory. On the other hand however, near neighbours West Calder made it to the quarter-finals at the first time of asking, drawn at home in all six ties played. West Calder started with a 5-1 victory over Kinleith, next up was Dunfermline, which resulted in a w/o. Round three ended with a 4-1 win over Brunswick, followed again by another w/o, this time against Stranraer. The fifth round ended in a 4-2 victory over Falkirk.

On the last day of the year 1881, West Calder played hosts to Busby side Cartvale, where they finally met their match, going down 5-3. A great start to the West Lothian cup campaign by all accounts.

THE BIGGER PICTURE

1881-82 Season saw Queens Park complete their hat-trick, and lift the trophy for the sixth time in the tournament's short history. West Calder's conquerors Cartvale went down heavily to Dumbarton, 11-2. The other semi-final saw Queens Park defeat Kilmarnock Athletic 3-2, before winning the final at Cathkin Park with a 4-1 victory after a 2-2 draw.

Season 1882-83 saw over 120 clubs enter the competition, but once again it was only West Calder and Addiewell who entered from the area even though both villages were just over the border in the neighbouring county of Midlothian. Once again West Calder were drawn at home against Kinleith, the game being recorded as a w/o in the home side's favour. Addiewell's home tie against Dunfermline also resulted in a w/o in their favour.

The second round saw Heart of Midlothian visit Addiewell. What should have been an interesting match for the village of Addiewell, turned out to be a total farce. The Addiewell club held their Annual Ball the evening before the match, which resulted in many players ending up a little the worse for wear. With only a few of the first team bothering to turn up, in the end the club had to muster together players with very little experience (it gives you an idea of the state of the game around this time). Under these conditions it could hardly be described as being a match; H Tierney, T Brown, J McCallum and D Dawson were the only regulars from the first team who took to the field, even the club captain was posted missing! With Hearts travelling out from Edinburgh, I'm sure they would have felt every bit disappointed, with the match ending up with a predictable score line of Addiewell 0 Heart of Midlothian 14, a sad end to what was to be Addiewell's last Scottish Cup result.

A few miles down the road saw Hibernian take on West Calder. A large attendance gathered for this match that turned out fast, furious and very rough play that resulted in a few injuries, and early on one of the

13

Hibernian's backs was so badly injured, he was unable to continue. With the rough play and slippery surface of the playing field, along with the very hostile crowd, the game was anything but pleasing, and many of the goals were hotly disputed from players and spectators alike. It was even mentioned that during the game there were too many umpires on the field of play commenting on various decisions. If the game had been left to those who were to officiate, the match itself would have been a far greater spectacle. In the end, the game finished West Calder 2 Hibernian 3.

THE BIGGER PICTURE

Semi final ties saw Dumbarton beat Pollockshields 5-0 after a protested match, with Vale of Leven defeating Kilmarnock Athletic 2-0 after a 1-1 draw. Dumbarton went on to lift the trophy at Hampden Park, winning 2-1, after a 2-2 draw.

1883-84 Season saw only one entrant into the competition, once again West Calder met Hibernian, and this time round the match was played in Edinburgh where Hibernian ran out comfortable 5-0 winners.

THE BIGGER PICTURE

Hibernian went on to reach the semi finals before going down 5-1 to Queens Park, and in the other semi final, Vale of Leven defeated Rangers 3-0. Queens Park were awarded the trophy as Vale of Leven failed to appear - they had asked for a postponement due to a family bereavement concerning one of their players, and they also stated that they had several players injured.

The 1884-85 Season saw Bo'ness enter the competition for the first time, with the Scottish Cup during this period being regionalised, due to the amount of entrants taking part in the competition. Therefore it was no surprise that Hibernian were to make another visit to West Lothian, with the Edinburgh side coming away with a 2-0 victory.

West Calder once again entered, which resulted in a home win over Norton Park by 3-0. The Second Round saw Dunblane visit West Calder, where again a large turnout of spectators gathered. The attendance could have been a lot higher if not been for a demonstration against the Franchise Bill in Bathgate, which saw a lot of the "Cauther" men descend on the town. Also reported in the local press at the time was the behaviour of the West Calder support, in which they had given themselves a bad name with their constant insults to players and officials during previous cup ties – at this time it seemed to be the trend around a lot of Scottish grounds! Never the less, the game kicked off at 4pm in what was a beautiful evening, with the playing surface in excellent condition. Like previous games, this match was also played at a fast and furious pace with a lot of rough play at times, resulting in West Calder ending the game with only ten men after right winger Watson was badly injured. This could not have happened at a worse time as Dunblane had just scored a few minutes earlier, the goal coming four minutes into the second half; this was to prove the only goal of the game and sent West Calder out of the cup.

THE BIGGER PICTURE

Hibernian once again made a semi final appearance, but failed to make the final after going down 3-2 to Renton. Vale of Leven defeated Cambuslang 3-1 after a 0-0 draw, before going down 3-1 to Renton at Hampden Park in the final.

1885-86 season saw the first Broxburn side compete in the national trophy, with the Irishmen from the village playing under the name of Broxburn Shamrock. The first game played in Broxburn saw Bo'ness come away with a 1-1 draw before hammering the Irishmen 5-1 at home. The only other match involving a county club resulted in a "walk over" in West Calder's favour against Borders club Newcastleton.

The second round saw Bo'ness hammer Norton Park 8-1 in a game which was ruined by heavy rain. West Calder received a bye, before being beaten 3-0 away to Wishaw Swifts in the third round. Bo'ness once again met Hibernian, this time at Easter Road; the Bo'ness side gave a good account for themselves, with the *Edinburgh Evening Express* being full of praise towards the West Lothian club even though they lost heavily 6-0. Sadly the end of the match was marred by crowd trouble.

THE BIGGER PICTURE

Renton once again defeated Hibernian in the semi finals, this time by a 2-0 score line, with Queens Park winning the other semi final tie against Third Lanark 3-0. Queens Park went on to lift the trophy for the eighth time defeating Renton 3-1 at Cathkin Park. This was also the season Arbroath made history defeating Bon Accord 36-0, amazingly on the same day Harp defeated Aberdeen Rovers 35-0.

A record amount of entries for the 1886-87 competition was made, and no fewer than eight county clubs took part. West Calder went down 3-1 at home to first time Scottish Cup entrants Armadale. Broxburn Shamrock lost 2-1 to Mossend Swifts, who were also making their debut in the competition.

Also making their mark for the first time was Broxburn side "Thistle" and South Queensferry side Belstane Birds, who played out to a 2-2 draw. This game was delayed twenty five minutes after the home side failed to appear, when the game finally got under way, "Birds had the better of the first half", leading 2-0 before "Thistle pulled two goals back after the interval". However, the Broxburn players had received rough treatment from the home support, at one stage the game being stopped for several minutes to clear the field of play. The replay at Broxburn watched by around 400 spectators saw Thistle stroll to an easy 4-1 victory.

Bellstane Birds Football Team 1890's © Mr R.N.Russell

Bo'ness travelled to Edinburgh to meet St. Bernards which saw the home side win 3-2. Also visiting Edinburgh was Bathgate side Durhamtown Rangers. The name seems a bit deceiving for this Irish Catholic side, who met Edinburgh's equivalent at Easter Road, and resulted in an easy passage into the next round for the home side, with a 6-1 victory. Incidentally it was "Rangers" who scored first and actually held the home side until half time.

The second round saw Heart of Midlothian visit the village of Broxburn in front of a crowd of 500-600. In a fairly even match, Hearts found the Broxburn defence, and goalkeeper Docherty, in top form, but Hearts opened the scoring midway through the first half, with Thistle managing to equalise before half time, when a long range effort came crashing off the underside of the bar before going in. The second half saw Hearts shoot down hill and more was expected of them, but in the end the Edinburgh side could only add one more goal, which was enough to see them into the next round. All in all Broxburn Thistle turned out a satisfying display.

Mossend Swifts had a home tie against Hibernian. This match caused quite a stir in the village, with many supporters from surrounding villages also lending their support, thus in turn a large amount of spectators were present, and in a hard fought match the game ended 1-1 after Mossend had taken an early lead. The replay at Easter Road saw Hibernian come out 3-0 winners.

Around this time it was common knowledge that both Hibernian and Heart of Midlothian were not particularly happy about playing West Lothian teams, as they felt themselves above them and would only participate when forced to play them in cup ties. This in turn added a bit more fight and aggression from the West Lothian clubs when playing against them.

The final tie of the round for the County clubs saw Armadale travel down to the Border town of Newcastleton, which was made worthwhile by beating the home side 5-1. It was recorded at the time that the 'Dale ended up 7s 6d out of pocket by the time the club had paid the referee and travelling expenses, it was not unknown for clubs to "scratch" simply because of the money involved for such a trip.

In the end Armadale ended up the only County side in the third round, with the prize being a trip to Powderhall to take on St. Bernards. With the game tied 2-2 at half time, Armadale keeper Love didn't have the best of games, and let in a further three in the second half to end the 'Dales first shot at the national competition.

THE BIGGER PICTURE

Hibernian eventually lifted the Scottish Cup after appearing in the previous three semi finals. The Edinburgh side defeated Dumbarton 2-1 at Hampden Park.

Into 1887-88 season, Broxburn Thistle travelled to Edinburgh to play holders Hibernian at Easter Road. As expected the game was pretty much one sided, with the home side taking a commanding lead before the break by the tune of five goals to nil. The second half was all Hibernian, but they failed to add to their score. At times Thistle did have some encouraging moments, in particular their defence, which was just as well considering the score line.

The other Broxburn side Shamrock went down 4-0 to Mossend Swifts at home, but protested over a player irregularity and were awarded the tie. Bo'ness defeated Leith Athletic at home 4-1 in front of a large crowd, and Armadale for the second consecutive season travelled to Powderhall to take on St. Bernards. Armadale were at full strength, but on the other hand, St. Bernards didn't have a keeper and played the match with one of their second eleven outfield players in goal. Even at that the 'Dale failed to take advantage and lost the tie 3-2.

Bathgate side Durhamtown Rangers now "Erin Rovers" played host to Bellstane Birds and won easily into the next round with a 5-0 victory. The final match of the round saw a home tie for West Calder against Edinburgh side Athenian and it was soon evident that the visitors were no match to the home side losing three goals in quick succession within the first ten minutes and eventually going down heavily by a 9-0 score line.

Bo'ness had home advantage of the second round tie against West Calder and they made it count with a 5-1 victory, but both sides had numerous chances in a game that swung from end to end. In the other matches

Broxburn Shamrock were drawn at home to St. Bernards, where they held the Edinburgh side to a commendable 1-1 draw before going out 4-1 in the replay. Erin Rovers lost heavily at home to Hibernian by a 6-0 score line.

Bo'ness advanced to the fourth round after defeating Lassodie 3-1. They then travelled to Alexandria to take on Vale of Leven Wanderers, both teams had chances to open their account, but the match remained goal-less up until the interval. Within five minutes of the restart however, Wanderers took the lead and for the remainder of the game it was the home side that dominated proceedings, but only managing to add one more goal, giving the home side a 2-0 victory.

THE BIGGER PICTURE

The record victory for a Scottish Cup final took place in this season, when Renton defeated Cambuslang 6-1; this feat was once again repeated in 1971-72 season when Celtic had the upper hand on Hibernian.

The first round of the 1888-89 Scottish Cup saw home side Armadale destroy Champfleurie by 12-0, the score line was hardly surprising as the visitors didn't even know who was to compose the team a couple of days before the match! This was Champfleurie's first taste of the national trophy, and with their lack of organisation they were certainly in for a stormy ride.

Another team from this area were Linlithgow Athletic, who also made their debut in the competition where they were drawn at home to Edinburgh side Adventurers. Early pressure paid off for the visitors, and by half time they found themselves comfortably leading by three goals at half-time. The second half saw Athletic start brightly, with Lees scoring two goals in quick succession. Adventurers eventually found their way and added another three goals before the final whistle ended with a 6-2 victory.

It was all happening in West Calder where Mossend Swifts proudly opened their new ground at Mossend Park. A lot of work was put in during close season which resulted in the pitch being in excellent condition, with a high perimeter fence surrounding the park, and pay boxes erected at the entrances. Without doubt Mossend Swifts were enjoying their "golden

19

years" and were easily the top side in the area, so much so that Robert Boyd and James Ellis were both capped for Scotland. Boyd securing two caps against Northern Ireland (1889) and Wales (1891), while Ellis was capped against Northern Ireland also (1892).

It was fitting to see top club Hibernian come to open the ground in a first round tie of the Scottish Cup, and since the draw was made supporters from both sides eagerly awaited the big day. Sadly on that day the weather was rather unforgivable, but it didn't stop what was at the time to be the largest attendance for a football match in the county.

Swifts had previously signed a couple of players from local rivals West Calder before the game (Gordon & Mackie). The game kicked off at 5pm with Swifts taking advantage of the wind, which proved to be a good call as the home team dominated early proceedings and deservingly took the lead through Inglis after only ten minutes, amidst tremendous cheering from the home support. Swifts had the better of the first half but did not add to their score. The start of the second half saw the Edinburgh side come more into the game but it was to be Swifts James Ellis who added a second goal. Once again to tremendous cheering, this brought a bit of fight into the Hibernian team who within minutes pulled one back to the delight of the Irish contingent in the ground. For the remainder of the game, Hibs did everything but score, giving Swifts a memorable 2-1 victory. As for Hibernian, this was the first time they had failed to get past the first round of the Scottish Cup, and as per usual the Hibs captain lodged a protest on the grounds of rough play, which was rightly dismissed.

Heart of Midlothian visited Bo'ness with three hundred of their support arriving by special train, to swell the gates to over a thousand. Bo'ness were well up for the task and matched their Edinburgh opponents throughout the game and were certainly unlucky to go down by a narrow 1-0 score line, the goal coming just before the half-time whistle.

Down the coast at South Queensferry, home side Bellstane Birds went down 3-2 to Norton Park. With the away side winning the toss, they took advantage of a strong wind and found themselves with a commanding 3-0 lead at half time. The home support were expecting a turnaround in the second half, but it took the team a full half an hour before they pulled a goal back, which gave Birds a little spirit. Although they did find the net again, they could not find that all important third to force a replay.

Erin Rovers won through to the next round defeating Leith Harp 6-0, but the match watched by a large support, was ruined due to constant rain. Broxburn Shamrock were due to meet West Calder at Broxburn, but owing to the referee not turning up the match was played as a friendly, which resulted in Shamrock winning 3-2. A couple of weeks later and more mismanagement this time due to Shamrock being unable to find a ground to play on, and eventually Uphall gave Shamrock permission to play in Uphall, but with West Calder already in Broxburn, they refused to travel the one mile up the road to play the game! The tie was eventually played the following week at West Calder and the home side went through to the next round winning 2-1 in a typically rough encounter.

The last remaining team Broxburn FC (name changed, formally known as Thistle) received a bye into the next round.

Into the second round and Broxburn had a home tie against Adventurers, while trailing 3-2 at half time, unfortunately the visiting keeper was unable to start the second half, which resulted in Broxburn playing against ten men in which they took full advantage by scoring seven second half goals, resulting in a 9-3 victory.

There was great excitement up in West Calder as they were drawn with local rivals Mossend Swifts. At the end of the day, favourites Swifts ran out easy 6-1 winners. Erin Rovers had two or three of their prominent players out for the visit to Tyncastle where Hearts at the end won through easily 4-0 to end the Bathgate's side's interest in the national trophy. Rovers had keeper Divers to thank for keeping the score to just four. Armadale received a bye into the next round.

The third round saw Armadale drawn away to Mossend Swifts, with Armadale sporting their new strip, blue and white vertical stripes. This clashed with Swifts, who in turn were forced to change as they were the home team, this didn't seem to have any effect on the home side, as they found themselves 2-0 up within five minutes. The 'Dale however managed to get back into the match and had levelled the scores by half time. The second half saw the fitter home side take command as lagging Armadale lost a further three goals, and Swifts deservedly running out 5-2 winners.

21

The second and final tie of round three for the West Lothian clubs saw Heart of Midlothian visit the Sports Fields in Broxburn, where a crowd of over 2000 gathered, 800 of whom had arrived from the capital. This was a match that Broxburn quite simply threw away. In a frantic start, and within the first ten minutes, Broxburn found themselves 2-0 up, with goals coming from Marr after five minutes, amidst tremendous cheering, with Russell adding a second four minutes later. Broxburn had many chances to increase their lead, but mainly down to excellent goalkeeping from McKay, Hearts kept the score line down. However, with nine minutes before the half time whistle, Hearts pulled one back. Into the second half and it was Broxburn who were doing all the pressing, again forcing McKay into numerous fine saves, and when it looked like Broxburn were going to hold out for a memorable win, Hearts broke away with ten minutes remaining, to force a replay.

At the end of the match the Broxburn support once again let their team down by attacking the Heart of Midlothian players as they left the field of play - stones had to be dodged and one player was severely kicked. When the club left their hotel a mob of supporters was still waiting on them issuing threats as the players left trembling with fear. *The Edinburgh Evening News blasted the home support, mentioning how disgraceful they had acted and were in danger of top Scottish teams refusing to play matches in the town*, this seemed at the time to be an ongoing problem.

A week later the sides met for the replay at Tyncastle, and around 400 Broxburn fans made the journey by special train to contribute to the 3000 attendance. In a poor match both teams had chances, but the first half ended up goalless, taking until the last 25 minutes before Hearts finally broke the deadlock and adding a second shortly after. Broxburn did come more into the game, but the score remained 2-0, leaving Broxburn to regret their missed chances from the first game.

This left Mossend Swifts the last remaining local side in the competition, who were drawn away to Uddingston, but Swifts simply blew away the Lanarkshire side in a match they dominated from start to finish, with Ellis getting a hat trick before Mackie added a fourth, with minutes remaining, Uddingston scored a consolation goal.

The fifth round saw Swifts travel to Boghead Park to take on one of the top West of Scotland sides at that time, Dumbarton. The game was made even more interesting for the fact that Mossend were the last remaining team not only from the county, but from the whole of the eastern district, as all Edinburgh sides had been knocked out the competition. All fifth round ties were pencilled in for the 24th November, but due to the condition of the Boghead pitch, the referee declared it unplayable for a cup tie and a friendly between the sides took place instead, that resulted in a draw. The following week the game went ahead where a large crowd had gathered, but heavy rain fell just before kickoff and continued throughout the match.

Dumbarton took advantage of the wind in the first half and it seemed their players adapted better to the muddy playing surface, resulting in a 2-0 half time lead. Midway into the second half however, Swifts pulled one back, to put some spark into the game. Swifts had equalised only for the referee to disallow and award a foul to Dumbarton. Taking advantage of this decision, they proceeded up field and added a final goal; Dumbarton finished the match with ten men, when one of their players went off the field after being kicked in the stomach. Even with ten men, the home side looked more likely to add to the score sheet.

Early West Calder photo, believed to be Mossend Swifts © Mrs Margaret Watt

THE BIGGER PICTURE

Semi final ties resulted in a 4-1 victory for Celtic over Dumbarton, while the other tie finished in Third Lanark's favour, defeating Renton 2-0. Third Lanark lifted the trophy with a 2-1 victory after protest, the first match which finished 3-0 to Thirds, known as the "snow final" as the pitch had a heavy covering of snow, so was correctly replayed.

It would be interesting to see if County clubs could improve on last season's exploits. Armadale were given a tough first round draw, but did not have their usual home advantage against Hibernian, as this was to be the first match played at Volunteer Park, as the 'Dale had previously been playing up the hill at Mayfield to the south of the village. The new pitch was not in the best of conditions but it was hoped it would improve through time. Hibernian brought along a large following by special train which swelled the gates, and was reported to be the largest attendance to date in the town.

The game itself looked dead and buried as Hibernian swept into a 3-0 lead, but just before half time, the home side pulled one back through Fleming. In a more equal second half, Fleming scored his and Armadale's second, a third goal to force for a replay was never found though, and Armadale went down 3-2.

Down the road at Boghead, Bathgate Rovers (Erin Rovers and Bathgate Volunteers combined) took the field against Champfleurie. It seems that problems arose during pre-season as for some reason or another, last season's Erin Rovers team had all but deserted them apart from the odd one or two, but the team still seemed to have that Irish influence as no fewer than four of the team came under the name of Kelly!. It seems Bathgate were struggling to field a team, as just before kickoff, only a couple of Bathgate players had entered the field of play with little as two dozen spectators around the ropes – in all fairness the above game at Armadale had taken centre stage. The game ended up 3-3 Champfleurie scoring in the first minute, but needing a late goal to force a replay. Due to Bathgate's problems, no replay took place and the Linlithgow side went into the hat for the next round.

Bo'ness travelled over to Mossend in what was expected to be a close match, with both clubs being holders of local cups at the time, and with previous games being close encounters. However, this did not go as planned with the home side thrashing the seasiders by six goals without reply. Another team also struggling was West Calder, at home to Broxburn they had difficulties raising a team, with most of them coming in from Junior side Addiewell Rovers's second eleven. As can be imagined, Broxburn had very few problems with a resounding 9-2 victory.

The final tie of the round saw Bellstane Birds record their first ever Scottish Cup win with a 6-3 victory over Norton Park, revenging last season's first round defeat. There was no Broxburn Shamrock in the draw as the struggling Irishmen with no ground or players, so the club finally called it a day.

The second round paired Hibernian and Mossend Swifts at Easter Road, which easily was the tie of the round for the eastern district, even though the Easter Road club had struggled over the past few seasons. Tensions were running high for this match as the previous week Hibernian were due to have played at Mossend in a benefit match for the sufferers of the Mauricewood Mining Disaster, but had failed to turn up. Rough play was therefore expected in the rematch with the referee warning both sets of players before the start of the match. The game finally got under way in front of 3000 spectators, but it wasn't until the twenty-fifth minute that Hibernian deservedly took the lead through McMahon. The same player increased Hibs lead within two minutes, but Swifts did pull one back before half time. Into the second half and Hibs continued to dominate and quickly scored a third and fourth goal, the homesters had chances to increase this lead, but it was Swifts who continued to press and pulled the score back to 4-3. With a couple of minutes remaining, Swifts scored again, only to the dismay of their players as the referee had blown his whistle seconds before the goal was scored for an infringement. Due to the confusion, both sets of supporters thought the goal had stood, much to the annoyance of the travelling support, when word finally filtered through that the goal was disallowed. Swifts lodged a protest but to no avail.

Bellstane Birds entertained Heart of Midlothian at South Queensferry, and as expected Hearts won the tie by 4-1, but didn't have it all their own way.

The Edinburgh Press once again voiced their disapproval at the rough tactics shown from the Queensferry side.

Leith Athletic visited Broxburn where a crowd of over one thousand witnessed another rough encounter. The following report was taken from *The Scottish Referee;-*

"BROXBURN TOO MUCH FOR LEITH ATHLETIC" The Leith Athletic got more than they bargained for at Broxburn in their Scottish tie with the club of that name. The Broxburn are almost invincible on their own ground and play a very desperate and forcible game., which though quite legitimate, is very dangerous to their opponents' and is apt to deprave the game in the eyes of most people. The Athletic have not met such opposition this season and at least six of their team can show injuries, which will long remind them of that little town. Each team scored two goals in the first half, and then the tug of war came in the second. No goals were scored, however, but towards the end the Broxburn looked all over winners. The injuries the Leith received prevented them from playing their usual game. The two Cuthbertsons' were the tower of strength to the Broxburn and Dewar, McQueen and Forest bore the brunt of the fight for Athletic.

The replay was at Bank Park and 400 Broxburn supporters saw their side go out the competition narrowly 2-1, Potter scoring Broxburn's only goal. Champfleurie were given a bye into the third round making them the last county club in the competition, thus earning a home tie against Heart of Midlothian. Champfleurie with the wind to their backs held Hearts for most of the first half, and only due to a goalkeeping error from Chambers the score would have been level at half time. During the second half however, it was Chambers who received all the credit in keeping the score to just five goals.

THE BIGGER PICTURE

Once again it was Queens Park's name that went on the trophy, after a 2-0 semi final win over Abercorn. Queens met Vale of Leven in the final after they had previously defeated Third Lanark 3-0. Queens beat Vale 2-1 after a 1-1 draw played at Ibrox.

Into season 1890/91 and three of the County sides Broxburn FC, Bo'ness and Mossend Swifts went straight into the second round due to walk-overs. The biggest concern was West Calder's non appearance against Broxburn, when it seemed the club had thrown in the towel. It turned out that only Bathgate Rovers joined the three into the next round, with a home win over Dunfermline Athletic, and in glorious sunshine Bathgate ran out 3-2 winners. By half time Rovers were 3-1 up, helped by a McCall double. Into the second half and Rovers fell away struggling to find their earlier form, a Baker own goal late on did cause a few anxious moments, but managed to hold out.

Armadale went down to Leith Athletic by the same score line at Bank Park, but this was mainly down to atrocious refereeing. Armadale started the game with new signing Potter from Broxburn and a large crowd from the Dale were also on hand to lend their support. Sadly the game was remembered for all the wrong reasons, as referee, a Mr McCulloch struggled with many important decisions. The Courier report at the time said "the sooner he is struck off, the better!" The worst error of the match happened right at the end when one of Athletics' players scored from the corner flag. The ball quite simply went out for a bye kick at the near post, but with all the noise from the home support, the referee who was some distance away, went with the crowd rather than his own instincts and the goal stood, but with all the other decisions that went against Armadale, the very least they deserved was a replay.

Linlithgow Athletic travelled over to Cowdenbeath with a weakened team due to many of their players opting to play cricket rather than football. Athletic "stuck in" well and found themselves narrowly losing 2-1, at the interval Paxton the scorer. The second half however the team totally caved in losing a further eight goals, resulting in a 10-1 defeat. The final game of the round saw Champfleurie visit Penicuik, where the home side won through to the next round with a 5-3 victory. Once again if not for Champfleurie's keeper, the score could have run into double figures. Bellstane Birds received a bye.

The second round and the goals continued to be scored at an alarming rate. First up was Broxburn FC's 5-2 victory over Clackmannan. Mossend Swifts defeated Jamestown away from home again by a 5-2 score line. Bathgate Rovers went one better against Dumbarton Union with a 6-2 victory; Rovers were on easy street leading 5-1 before the interval, with Gardner scoring a hat trick.

With the Forth Rail Bridge being built at that time, many Bellstane Birds players worked on constructing the bridge. Regrettably a few of the players lost their lives, and sadly this was to happen days before their cup tie with Bo'ness. Out of respect, the game was postponed and eventually played a fortnight later resulting in a 7-0 victory to Bo'ness.

The third round paired the County clubs, with Bathgate Rovers receiving a home tie against Broxburn FC, while Bo'ness were drawn at home to Mossend Swifts. With Broxburn having cup success locally, it was no surprise that scouts from all over were homing in on the players, which resulted in the town losing more of less their entire team, apart from goalkeeper, Docherty. The team that faced Rovers was more or less Broxburn junior side Cardross Swifts, with one player even remarking before kick-off that he had not played in five years, so it was to be no surprise that Rovers won easily 6-0. When the sixth goal was scored near the end, many supporters began to leave the ground, disgusted with the match by players showing very little urgency, this contributed to one of the dullest matches ever seen at Boghead.

In front of a large turnout of spectators, Bo'ness and Mossend Swifts could not be separated in this exciting tie, which ended 1-1. The replay at West Calder was different altogether, where Swifts simply crushed their opponents 9-1.

Into the fourth round both Mossend and Bathgate finally met their match, and Mossend once again made the trip west to take on a very strong Dumbarton side, in fact a side that was to reach the final and also win the very first Scottish League (jointly with Rangers). In a rain lashed Boghead, the game was barely seconds old when Swifts took the lead through Inglis, but within five minutes Dumbarton had reversed the scores and were leading 2-1. Dumbarton continued to dominate and were unlucky on several occasions not to put the tie beyond Mossend. During this pressure however, Swifts broke away and scored two goals in quick succession to regain the lead. With the game being played at a very fast pace, Dumbarton once again took the lead by scoring three times before half time, taking the score to 5-3. Midway into the second half Dumbarton made it six, before completing the score with a seventh and final goal, with fifteen minutes remaining. One of the Ellis brothers collided with one of the Dumbarton backs, which resulted in the later being taken off the pitch. Things began to boil over when a further three Dumbarton players were injured, resulting in a pitch invasion by the angry home support. The pitch was eventually cleared and the result stood; Dumbarton 7 Mossend Swifts 3.

In the other tie, Rovers travelled to Underwood Park in Paisley to take on Abercorn, another founder member of the Scottish League and a team who had scored twenty four goals in the previous three rounds, so it was no surprise to see Bathgate's defence under prolonged pressure. This resulted in the home side taking a five goal lead before half time. With the game all but won, Abercorn played the game out at a relaxing pace, scoring a further three goals in the process. Rovers on the other hand sat back defending their goal, keeping down any further scoring, resulting in an 8-0 defeat. At close of the tie, Rovers protested on the grounds of darkness and of the Abercorn team turning up late, but all to no avail.

THE BIGGER PICTURE

Dumbarton met Abercorn in the semi-finals, winning 3-1. The other semi-final tie saw Heart of Midlothian defeat Third Lanark 4-1. Hearts went on to lift the cup scoring the only goal of the game at Hampden Park. As mentioned previously, the first Scottish League was played for and shared by Rangers and Dumbarton.

The start of 1891-92 season the Scottish Cup took a different format and preliminary rounds were introduced, with the Scottish League now into its second year. The member clubs didn't have to join the Scottish Cup until the latter rounds along with last year's semi finalists, with only the first preliminary round being regionalised. The top game of the first round in the district, the one which certainly caught most people's eye was the local derby between Armadale and Bathgate Rovers at the Volunteer Park. Rovers took advantage of the strong wind, and an own goal by Lafferty gave the visitors the lead after 15 minutes, and before the interval Clark and McCall had increased the visitors lead. The match up until that point had been littered with fouls. Into the second half, it was now Armadale who were shooting downhill and also with the wind advantage. Within 15 minutes of the restart, Armadale were on level terms and continued to play the better of the match, but failed to find that decisive fourth goal. The following week and Bathgate with home advantage deservedly went through to the next round with a 3-0 victory in front of 1500 spectators.

Broxburn FC were drawn at home to Raith Rovers, with the visitors arriving half an hour late. The Kirkcaldy side won the toss and took advantage of the strong breeze, after all the early pressure; Rovers could not break down the home defence, with Broxburn keeper Walker in excellent form. As half time approached, Broxburn were having their best spell, and Chambers opened the scoring with a long low drive, half-time Broxburn 1 Raith Rovers 0. Into the second half it was Broxburn who continued to dominate the game. However, with fifteen minutes remaining, Rovers scored against the run of play, Bogie scoring from another long range shot. Broxburn were not to be outdone and with less than five minute remaining, Chambers scored his and Broxburn's second goal amidst great cheering. Before the final whistle the home side were unlucky not to increase their lead on several occasions, but in the end went into the second round draw with a 2-1 victory.

Bo'ness and Linlithgow Athletic travelled to Fife to take on Dunfermline Athletic and Burntisland Thistle respectively. Bo'ness went down 4-0, all Dunfermline's goals coming in the first half. Up the coast in Burntisland, Linlithgow had more luck through also losing four goals, managed to reply with six.

Mossend Swifts travelled to Davidson Mains to take on Muirhouse Rovers, where they had no difficulty in reaching the next round, with an easy 7-1 victory. The home side's consolation goal arrived with only a couple of minutes remaining from the new penalty kick rule. Finally Broxburn Shamrock were back on the scene, with Lochgelly United scratching, they marched on into the second round.

The second round produced goals galore, with the highest number being eleven, as Kilsyth club Smithston Hibernian crushed Linlithgow Athletic 11-1 at their Haugh Park ground, which incidentally was in a deplorable state. Another twelve goals were scored when Alva went down 9-3 at home to Mossend Swifts in a match that was ruined by strong wind and rain.

The weather was similar at Boghead Park where Bathgate Rovers were up against Slamannan Rovers in front of 600 spectators. Bathgate attacked the goal towards the railway end and with a strong wind in their favour, found themselves five goals up within quarter of an hour. Two more were added before half time with another shortly after the restart. Bathgate's Thomas Baillie scored no fewer than five of the eight goals, an own goal by Brown gave Slamannan a consolation resulting in an 8-1 final score line.

The only other County club to have home advantage were Broxburn Shamrock who entertained Campsie at Shamrock Park, where the wind and rain again played a large part in the game. Shamrock took advantage of the weather conditions in the first half taking a 5-2 lead, barely into the second half and Shamrock added a sixth, shortly after that goal, the game was stopped due to torrential rain. When the game restarted, the wind and rain had somewhat died down, and Campsie had scarcely the same advantage. The visitors did manage to pull the scores back to 6-4 before the full time whistle sounded. At the end Campsie protested the match on the basis that they didn't get a fair advantage as far as the weather conditions went, and were awarded a replay. It would appear that back then , more so than today's modern game that the wind element would have more say to the outcome of matches mainly due to the wide open spaces and very little shelter compared to the stands and terracing of today. Campsie's appeal was in vain though as Shamrock once again came out on top, this time with a 3-1 victory.

The final tie of the round saw Broxburn FC travel out to Duntocher, near Clydebank, to take on home town team Harp. After a long train journey, the Broxburn team then had two miles to walk from the station to the ground in pouring rain. On arrival the club was greeted with a very poor turnout of spectators and a playing field where the home side would have considerable advantage being used to playing on such a sloping surface. Broxburn decided to hit downhill and lead 1-0 at the interval. The second half and Broxburn still managed to create changes, however, Harp then took advantage of the slope and ended up 4-2 winners.

Over a thousand spectators' gathered at Boghead Park where Rovers entertained Falkirk, in what turned out to be a fascinating game, where ten goals were shared. Falkirk looked home and dry with less than 15 minutes remaining, leading 5-2. Rovers however had other ideas and pressed hard

31

for the last quarter of the game, scoring three goals to force a deserved replay. Nobody for a minute thought that Rovers could possibly travel over to Falkirk and beat them on their own turf at Brockville, however the town of Bathgate were in high spirits during the week after their excellent comeback, with the Rovers committee organising a special train for two hundred Bathgate followers, but by the end of the day, that figure had nearly doubled with hopeful supporters accompanying the team. Falkirk certainly didn't seem the same team from the previous Saturday and seemed quite content on committing foul after foul. Bathgate however continued where they had left off with Baillie and Dunlop scoring before half time. Seven minutes after the break Dunlop wrapped the tie up grabbing his second and Bathgate's third. Falkirk's fouling got even worse and Prey was ordered off for deliberately kicking Rover's McCall in the chest. Bathgate with the extra player comfortably saw off the remainder of the match to record a memorable victory of 3-0.

After the match, the Bathgate contingent made their way to the station full of voice, with nothing heard but "Good old Rovers!" The train finally left Falkirk shortly after seven where the singing continued the whole journey, and the train arrived home to a large rejoicing crowd who had gathered. It was a night that was seldom seen in Bathgate and the team were well received all around town, with the remainder of the night being spent in their headquarters, The Masons Arms, in a very merry manner.

Mossend Swifts also visited Falkirk to take on East Stirlingshire, in an exciting match, which went from end to end. The home side won by the odd goal in nine! After defeating Linlithgow Athletic, Smithston Hibernian were once again drawn at home against a County club, this time Broxburn Shamrock, in what turned out to be bad tempered affair. There was no repeat of the 11-1 thrashing handed out in the previous round, as Shamrock took a 2-0 lead before the home side pulled one back in the second half. After that both teams had chances but the game ended 2-1 to the visitors.

Shamrock received a bye in the final preliminary round, while Bathgate entertained Clydebank at Boghead. Due to Clydebank arriving late, the game finished in semi-darkness. Early in the game it could easily be seen that Rovers were by far the better team and by their half-time lead of 2-0. Clydebank did pull one back at the beginning of the second half but Rovers continued to have the bulk of the play and added a further three goals resulting in a 5-1 victory. So good was Bathgate's form that agents from top English clubs were beginning to appear in the town.

First round proper and Bathgate made the trip west to Glasgow (Govan) to take on Linthouse, and in what was a poor attendance, the Bathgate "Bairns" easily outnumbered the home support. Once again Bathgate were the underdogs, but Rovers surprised everyone with another tremendous performance, there was little more than two minutes on the clock when Kennedy opened the scoring. A minute later, "Ginger" Murnin added a second where a single handed piece of dribbling saw him waltz round the home defence before tucking the ball away into the corner. Before the half time whistle, the game was as good as over, as Baillie added a third with Kennedy and Murnin again increasing the tally. The second period was played at a relaxing pace with Murnin completing his hat trick late on – final score Linthouse 0 Bathgate Rovers 6. Sadly Rovers would have struggled to clear their expenses as half the gate receipts amounted to a mere 2s 2d (11p).

In the other tie Broxburn Shamrock had home advantage over Northern (Glasgow). A heavy frost during the night made the game doubtful, but with a large crowd gathering and a good few from Glasgow, the game went ahead, and an entertaining first half saw Shamrock lead 4-2, with a further three goals in the second half completing the scoring, rounding off a 7-2 victory.

Both Rovers and Shamrock could not have asked for a better second round draw, even though Bathgate were again drawn away, with another train journey through to Glasgow. The club were to meet Scottish Cup specialists Queens Park at Hampden. Shamrock on the other hand had home advantage against Scottish Cup holders Heart of Midlothian. The Hampden tie saw a fair crowd travelling from Bathgate, many of which were now beginning to believe this could be Rovers year.

The Bathgate team consisted of the following; Thornton, Bryce, McPhee, Kelly, Donnelly, W.Murnin, J.Murnin, Baillie, Kennedy, McCall and Fleming.

In a one sided affair, Queens Park dominated much of the first half but found keeper Thornton in fine form, and by the time the whistle sounded for half time, all Queens had to show for their efforts was a solitary strike from Hamilton. Surprisingly enough in a more evenly balanced second half, Queens Park still managed to add a further five goals to round off the scoring; Queens Park 6 Bathgate Rovers 0. Probably the most pleasant part of the tie for Rovers was the way they were treated after the match by the Queens officials. A company of around fifty sat down for supper, the Queens Park chairman warmly complimented Rovers followed by a musical programme, with the Bathgate lads singing their hearts out. Soon after the team left to catch their train back to Bathgate, with half the £17 gate money – a big difference from the 2s 2d received from the previous round.

Heart of Midlothian ran a special train from Edinburgh out to Broxburn and it was quite evident that the Tynecastle outfit had the majority of the support within Shamrock Park. Hearts were at full strength while Shamrock was minus their captain Mechan, reason being a dispute over pay while the player had been off work. Shamrock's team were as follows;

Gordon, John & Jas McCabe, Hughes, Bryne, J McCann, Brady, Cannon, Miller, E McCann and Gribbins.

In a lively first half, both teams produced many chances with Hearts making the most of them by taking a 3-0 lead. Before half time however, the "greens" managed to pull themselves back into contention, narrowing the score line to just the one goal. The second half saw Hearts pressure rewarded with two further goals which seemed to wrap up the tie, but the home side had other ideas and had most of the play until the end of the game, scoring another two and just missing out on that all important fifth, which would have earned them a replay at Tynecastle. This was easily the best display to date in the Scottish Cup by the Linlithgowshire clubs, and certainly brought a lot of recognition to the area.

THE BIGGER PICTURE

Celtic defeated Rangers 5-3 in the first semi final, while the following week Queens Park and Renton saw out a 1-1 draw, before Queens finally progressed into the final with a 3-0 win. The final played at Ibrox Park saw Celtic lift the trophy, which was to be the first of many, defeating Queens Park 5-1. This final had been replayed following crowd trouble, which Celtic had also won 1-0.

After Bathgate Rovers and Broxburn Shamrock's fine run in the "Scottish" the previous season, both clubs had relatively easy home ties and progressed into the second round, Rovers with five changes saw off Edinburgh side Adventurers, with ease 7-1. Shamrock on the other hand disposed of a poor Bonnyrigg Rose side 5-0. The game that created the most excitement in the county was the meeting between Mossend Swifts and Broxburn FC. This game resulted in a 2-1 victory for Mossend, although Broxburn had the bulk of the play they failed to get the better of the Swifts defence.

Linlithgow Athletic also made it into the hat, with a 4-1 win over Muirhouse Rovers at Captains Park. Athletic all the same, had goalkeeper Charlie Wilson to thank for the convincing score line and taking them into the next round.

Armadale travelled over to Fife to take on Dunfermline Athletic, and it appears before the game the 'Dale were struggling to put a team together, in the end juniors from local sides made up the numbers, so it was to be quite a surprise when Armadale recorded a 4-1 victory. The final tie of the round saw Bo'ness go down to Polton Vale at Newtown Park by the odd goal in seven!

The second preliminary round saw all clubs apart from Broxburn Shamrock stumble out of the competition. First up was Bathgate Rovers who travelled to Alexandria to take on the "unknowns" Levendale. Rovers got off to the worst possible starts, before they had time to settle they found themselves 1-0 down in under two minutes. The game was littered with bad refereeing decisions throughout the match, mainly against the Rovers. With less than ten minutes remaining and the match sitting tight at 2-1, the home side added a third, which was hotly disputed by the Rovers players, in particular Bryce, who in turn chased the referee down the pitch before grabbing him by the neck. Bryce was ultimately ordered off the field. The final minute of play saw Levendale add to the misery scoring a fourth and final goal.

Once again a County club made the journey west to take on Duntocher Harp on their infamous sloping pitch, this time Mossend Swifts, like

35

Broxburn FC the previous season, came away empty handed in a 2-1 defeat. Armadale travelled over to Clackmannan, with the 'Dale winning the toss, they took advantage of a strong wind and by the interval found themselves leading 3-1. The tables turned however, with Clackmannan dominating most of the second half, they managed a further three goals to record a 4-3 victory.

Linlithgow Athletic entertained Gairdoch where both teams shared six goals. Athletic were leading 3-1 at half time, mainly due to a strong wind. The replay at Carronshore saw Gairdoch record a 6-3 victory against a disorganised Linlithgow side.
The Broxburn Shamrock v Bridge of Allan game resulted in a walk over in Shamrock's favour; this set the Irishmen up with a home tie against East Stirlingshire. Shamrock were rather unfortunate to be trailing 1-0 at the interval, having most of the play. The home side seemed to have equalised only for the referee to chalk the goal off, indicating that the ball had indeed went by the post. This was quite a common problem before the introduction of nets. The second half however, was all Shamrock and they turned their superiority into goals, ending up with a 3-1 victory. Near the end of this match the game was stopped on no less than three occasions by the referee, having to warn both sets of players over their rough play.

The fourth and final round of the preliminary ties, Shamrock once again had home advantage, this time against Partick Thistle. With a slight wind blowing, Shamrock took advantage and by the half time whistle had the bulk of play and a 2-1 lead. In a more evenly matched second half, a replay in Glasgow seemed on the cards, as the sides were tied at 3-3. With less than a minute remaining Hughes with one of his speciality throw-ins landed in the goalmouth and after a scrimmage, the ball was forced over the line. Thistle players protested but the goal was allowed to stand, with the final whistle sounding seconds later, Shamrock went into the first round proper of the competition.

Shamrock made the trip north to take on a Dunblane side that had also produced a few fine displays to get this far in the competition. Shamrock however were in great form and strolled into a 3-0 half time lead. Into the second half, chances were created at both ends, but there was no further scoring as Shamrock proceeded into the next round.

A home tie against Stirling's Kings Park, in what was reported as being one of the toughest matches ever played at Shamrock Park at that time, but once again it was to be the "greens" that came out on top with yet another 3-0 victory. Brady was most instrumental in the Shamrock attacks, setting up the first goal and scoring two in the second half. Once again the match was protested on the grounds that one of the crossbars was three quarters of an inch too low, this claim was rejected and Shamrock marched into the third round.

Yet another home tie for Shamrock, this time against Scottish League side St. Mirren, a side that were to finish off the season in third place, below only Celtic and Rangers. Brady continued where he left off and put Shamrock ahead with less than a minute on the clock, St. Mirren came more into the game and equalised, but before half time, a mistake by the Saints keeper let Brady in to score his second goal and give Shamrock a 2-1 interval lead. Saints dominated early proceedings in the second half and turned the game around to their favour, taking a 3-2 lead. Minutes later O'Bryne equalised and with only five minutes remaining Millar scored the winner to give Shamrock a 4-3 victory.

As per usual the Paisley men protested, this time they reported the language used by the Shamrock support. Again claims were dismissed and Shamrock booked a place in the Scottish Cup semi finals – a fantastic achievement for the County team, also considering that Shamrock were only resuscitated a couple of seasons previously.

This is how the Courier reported on the game;

BROXBURN SHAMROCK v QUEENS PARK

For two seasons in succession, Linlithgowshire has been represented in the final stages of the Scottish Cup. Last season the Bathgate Rovers met the Queens Park in the second round at Hampden Park and were defeated by 6 goals to nil. After playing what was the press characterised as a "peculiar" game; peculiar so far that they held the famous eleven firmly, till about twenty minutes off the expiry of the game, and then let the Queens win as they choose. This year Broxburn Shamrock took the place of the Rovers and winning from such teams as Campsie, East Stirlingshire, Kings Park and St. Mirren, entered the semi final of the cup by meeting the finalist at Hampden last Saturday. It was a new experience for most of the players to play before such a crowd, but if we take the demeanour of that crowd as a criterion of its sympathy, we fancy that the team of green jerseys who appeared last Saturday against the famous Spiders, received and deserved the plaudits of the seven odd thousand who witnessed the match. The day was an ideal one for football, both from a players and spectators standpoint, and when the Shamrock appeared on the field, the reception they got merited much of the fairness of the crowd. The slight wind that blew was taken advantage of by the ground team and when Mr Johnston, Kings Park (whose doings will not be noted afterwards) gave the word for commencement of hostilities, it was seen that the game would be a hard one. Of course the visitors were shown up very much regarding their want of success, as exemplified by "gallery work" done by Gulliland and Waddell, but when it came to defence by the Shamrock, that section of the game was in very capable hands. The strong kicking of Docherty and McCabe at the back and the smart and sure work of Walker in goal were prominent features, which were quickly appreciated by the crowd, and often heartedly applauded. Often as not, the shots that were sent to the goalkeeper were negotiated in smart returns, and we can safely conjuncture that only for the grand defence the goal score would have been high. However, for a long time, the Shamrock were hemmed in at all points, and after 25 minutes play, Hamilton from a pass from Guilliland scored the first point for Queens. This was received by an outburst of cheering which seemed to have an echo in the hearts of the Shamrock, who played up remarkably hard after this reverse. The game, however, was not what should be looked upon as fast; several shady and disagreeable tactics being introduced on both sides, and the Referee was occasionally at fault at not using his prerogative, which he might have done to advantage on many occasions. The game deteriorated, and the frequent fouls tended to raise the temper of the onlookers, who showed their disapprobation by loud howls and hisses. The second goal for Queens was got through the same style of piloting the ball down the filed by the right wing and centring. The second half of the game was harder played, the visitors getting more into the lay of the land and holding their own to such an extent that they scored twice, and although the ground team also put in another two goals, the game was far more even. Near to the close of the game, the Shamrock were pressing hard and almost scored just as the whistle blew. An unfortunate accident happened to Lambie who collided with Docherty; he

38

had to be assisted off the field and was unable to resume play in the second half.

This was also taken from the *Scottish Sport;*

The Queens Park officials and players are almost unanimous in describing the Broxburn Shamrock as the roughest team that have ever been seen at Hampden. They discovered the key to the success of the miners on Saturday, and know now how too many good clubs were overcome. They believe, had they been sent to the circumscribed limits of the Shamrock's pitch, they would not have had room to escape; they would have been hammered and then defeated. The Shamrock made a mistake in so exposing themselves.

At the end of the day, Shamrock went down 4-2 to the eventual winners, but their feat of making the last four of the national competition; it wasn't repeated until 2001 that a West Lothian team did likewise, when "new" club Livingston went down 3-0 to Hibernian at Hampden.

THE BIGGER PICTURE

Celtic defeated St. Bernards 5-0 in the other semi final. The final between Celtic and Queens Park was replayed because of the condition of the pitch, which Celtic had won 1-0. The replayed game saw Queens Park win 2-1, both games played at Ibrox. This turned out to be Queens Park's last success in the National Trophy, the club continuing to oppose professionalism were gradually left behind, and the talent which flocked to them in the early days were now seeking other clubs where their fortune could be found.

The 1893-94 season got under way and Armadale had no problems gunning down the First Argyll and Sutherland Highlanders, in a warm sunny day. The soldiers based at Edinburgh Castle fielded a weakened team and were no match for the 'Dale, who ran out 8-1 winners.

Mossend Swifts were also in a goal scoring mood, when they put nine goals past Adventurers without reply. Swifts were strongly represented with many of their ex-players returning with the exception of the Hogg brothers, who were still at Tyncastle.

39

Bathgate Rovers and Bathgate Athletic joined forces to form a new club, under the banner of just plain Bathgate FC. Their first game resulted in a draw 0-0 against Kirkcaldy. The replay over in Fife saw Bathgate go down to the odd goal in five, Kirkcaldy helped along with a dodgy penalty decision.

Bo'ness went down 4-3 away to Bonnyrigg Rose, while Polton Vale defeated Uphall 5-2. Linlithgow Athletic scratched to Lochgelly United and finally Broxburn FC received a bye into the next round.

All the County clubs were away from home for the second round of the preliminary ties, Broxburn travelled through to Easter Road to take on league leaders of the newly formed Second Division, Hibernian FC, but a poor Broxburn side were easily brushed aside and went down 5-0.

Armadale visited Grangemouth and also suffered heavily losing 6-2. Finally for the second year running Mossend Swifts travelled to Duntocher, where the home side were now playing it seems at Fore Park, rather than their notorious sloping pitch at the previous St. Helena Park. Harp got off to a flying start with two quick goals, however, within thirty minutes had two players injured, and although they continued to play for the duration of the game, it proved too much of a handicap for the home side as Swifts went on to record a 5-2 victory.

The third round, and Mossend Swifts were drawn against Kirkcaldy away, but somehow the team managed to miss their train connection in Edinburgh and arrived late for the match. The Fife side tried to claim the game, but it did finally go ahead and ended up three goals apiece, the replay at Mossend resulted in a walk-over to Swifts.

A home tie in the fourth preliminary round saw Second Division side Port Glasgow Athletic visit Swifts, with a good gathering of supporters witnessing a stiffly contested match. Swifts were seconds away from a memorable victory when Athletic forced home a second goal to equalise and take the game to a replay.

Many were optimistic that Swifts could still win the tie as long as they still played with the same enthusiasm as the first game. This was not to be the case however, the first twenty minutes or so was evenly matched but by half time, Athletic were leading by a 4-1 score line. Play was rough in the second half, but with the league side firmly in control, they added a further five goals, with Swifts also finding the net, resulting in a 9-3 victory, sending Swifts tumbling out of the cup.

With Broxburn Shamrock reaching the semi final stages the previous season, they automatically entered the first round proper of the competition and were given a home draw against Arbroath. By the interval things looked good for Shamrock, as they coasted to a 3-1 lead. Arbroath however scored twice in a minute midway through the second half to draw level, both goals mainly down to goalkeeping errors from Keast. Worse was to follow for the Shamrock keeper, when he was ordered off for rough play, any lingering hopes of Shamrock taking anything out of the game were now dashed, with Arbroath having that extra man advantage, they soon made it count by scoring five goals in rapid succession and ending Shamrock's cup run prematurely. No more goals were scored with the game ending 8-3 to the visitors.

THE BIGGER PICTURE

The semi-final ties kept the Old Firm apart (see, it was even happening back then!!). Rangers needed a replay to dispose of 'Queens Park 3-1 after a 1-1 draw. The other semi-final saw Celtic score five against Third Lanark in an entertaining eight goal thriller. The final played at Hampden Park saw Rangers win the first Old Firm final 3-1, where no fewer than nine internationals were playing in the Rangers jersey.

Professionalism was beginning to poison the ranks of County football; local clubs were struggling, with "main players", and Armadale and Broxburn FC calling it a day. Many footballers had been lost to top English clubs over the past few years as they were tempted down south with big pay deals. Now with top Scottish clubs doing likewise, it was no surprise to see County teams struggle. One local reporter at that time suggested that West Lothian clubs should form two professional teams, splitting the district in half, with Broxburn, Linlithgow and Bo'ness making up one team, and West Calder, Bathgate and Armadale forming the other. This way it would stop the city teams using the County as training grounds and picking off the top players. This idea as you could imagine never got off the ground.

The shock of the first round was surely Bathgate's defeat at Linlithgow. Close season everyone had tipped Bathgate to be the team to beat in the County, but their high hopes were soon dashed as Athletic swept aside a poor Bathgate side 4-1. Uphall travelled down to the Borders and easily disposed of Kelso 5-0. Further victories for Bo'ness were 4-1 over Bonnyrigg Rose, Mossend Swifts 3-1, a win over Lochgelly United and a massive 11-1 victory for Broxburn Shamrock over Loch Rangers (Leavenseat, Fife) saw five of the County clubs safely into the next round.

Shamrock travelled to Camelon, where the home side came out on top with a 3-1 win. Uphall also went out, losing 4-2 at home to Raith Rovers. Goalkeeping errors from the Uphall keeper was the main reason the home side didn't take anything out of the game.

Mossend Swifts had a fine 2-0 home win over Kilsyth Wanderers, but once again a protest was lodged on the grounds that the playing field was improperly marked, parts of the field were overgrown and in these areas, the touchlines were hardly visible - the appeal was won. This seemed to inspire the Swifts and in determined manner, they strolled to a 5-0 victory in the replayed match.

The final tie of the round for the County clubs produced a local derby between Linlithgow Athletic and Bo'ness. There was great interest from both towns for this match, a healthy attendance of over 2000 was on hand to witness the occasion. It took until thirty minutes before the first goal was scored, coming for Athletic through Bowman. The goal seemed to inspire the home side as they pressed hard for the remainder of the half, but failed to increase their lead. Within a minute of the restart, Bo'ness were level, and then two goals in quick succession gave the visitors a 3-1 lead. Athletic did pull one back, but in the closing minutes another two goals were scored to record a fine 5-2 victory for Bo'ness.

Bo'ness received a bye into the next round, Mossend travelled to Clackmannan. Although there was very little between the sides, it was Swifts who took their chances and went in at half time 2-0 up. The second half was ruined by torrential rain, Clackmannan scored shortly after the restart, but Mossend found the net for a third in the last ten minutes to enter the fourth round.

Swifts this time round were given a bye, which meant they were now into the first round proper of the cup. Bo'ness were given a home tie against top Ayrshire club Ayr Parkhouse. In a fairly even first half Bo'ness found themselves 1-0 down. Apart from the opening few minutes of the second period, where Parkhouse increased their lead, the second half belonged to Bo'ness, who were rather unfortunate not to have won the tie, as they managed to claw back the deficit, numerous chances were had, but in the end Bo'ness had to settle for a 2-2 draw.

Leaving Bo'ness by the 8.25am train, the players plus fifty supporters made their way to Ayr. Both teams made changes from the first game, Parkhouse arrived fifteen minutes late and even commenced with only ten players on the park. The playing surface of Beresford Park was also questioned, the field being covered by rather long yielding turf, the sloping pitch also had, what was described as several nasty "hillocks", and to crown it all there was a strong wind blowing from goal to goal. When the game finally got underway, Bo'ness took advantage of the driving wind and opened the scoring within a minute, this though was to be the only goal for the visitors as the Parkhouse defence were in outstanding form. At the end of the day Bo'ness went down 6-1, the result does not do them justice, as there was never five goals between the sides.

This left Mossend Swifts to carry the banner for the County into the first round proper of the Scottish Cup, their reward was an away tie against Second Division Motherwell. All the goals came in the first forty five minutes, and although Motherwell had the bulk of the second half, they failed to secure that second goal and the game ended up in Swifts favour 2-1.

It was now Mossend's turn to travel down the west coast to take on Ayr Parkhouse. The game drew the largest attendance that had been seen in the ground all season. The home side once again had its rear guard to thank, as Swifts had the better of the ninety minutes, but with just under five minutes remaining and the scores tied at 1-1, the home side scored twice unexpectedly to record a 3-1 win and send the Swifts out of the national competition.

THE BIGGER PICTURE

The semi final tie between Dundee and Renton took three attempts, before Renton marched into the final 1-1, 3-3, 3-0. The other tie was an all Edinburgh affair between St. Bernards and Heart of Midlothian, with the match needing a replay after a 0-0 draw. Saints scored the only goal of the game in the replay at Logie Green. St. Bernards lifted the trophy for the first and only time defeating Renton 2-1 at Ibrox Park.

1895-96 season saw a new format, where the Scottish Qualifying Cup was introduced. Instead of having preliminary rounds, the last sixteen of the competition entered the Scottish Cup proper, along with the First Division sides, the competition was still played to a close, and like previous early rounds of the "Scottish", the draw was sectioned into geographical areas.

Football in the County at this time was at a low ebb, with only five sides entering the Qualifying Cup, none of them managing to get by the second round, where in turn no team made it into the Scottish Cup proper.

Bathgate had the most convincing result revenging the previous season's defeat at the hands of Linlithgow with a 5-0 win. Uphall went down 5-2 against Kirkcaldy, while Kelso scratched to Bo'ness and Mossend Swifts received a bye.

The second round saw all three teams drawn away from home and also ended their interests in the competition. Mossend went down 3-2 at Stirling against Kings Park, where a fire broke out in the grandstand during play. Swifts players put this down as the reason of losing the tie, with Kirkcaldy knocking out Bo'ness 4-0. The heaviest defeat saw Bathgate go down 7-0 to Stenhousemuir.

THE BIGGER PICTURE

Hearts returned last season's semi final defeat against holders St. Bernards by the same score 1-0, while Hibernian defeated Renton 2-1 to set up a Hibs v Hearts final, played at Logie Green. This was to be the only time ever a Scottish Cup final was played outside Glasgow, Hearts going on to lift the trophy with a 3-1 win.

1896-97 saw no fewer than seven county clubs enter the Qualifying Cup. Armadale were back on the senior stage; more or less it seems that the juniors from the town had made the step up, their first round tie at home finished Armadale Volunteers 3 Broxburn Shamrock 1. Bo'ness and West Calder both scratched to Lochgelly United and Bathgate respectively. Mossend lost at home to Raith Rovers 2-1, and the final tie of the round saw Linlithgow Athletic scratch to Penicuik Athletic. This left only Bathgate and Armadale in the competition. Selkirk scratched to the former while Penicuik disposed of the Volunteers 4-0. The third round saw Bathgate easily through to the next round 6-2 against Cameronians, a fourth and fifth round bye followed by a 5-1 defeat in Aberdeen against Orion, but this was enough to see them into the first round of the "Scottish". Bathgate slumped 5-0 away to Blantyre to end another dismal year in the Scottish Cup.

THE BIGGER PICTURE

Plenty of goals were scored in both semi final ties, Dumbarton defeating Kilmarnock 4-3, while Morton went down 7-2 to Rangers. There was no let up in the final as Rangers saw off Dumbarton 5-1. Non league side Arthurlie shocked First Division Celtic with a 4-2 home win in the first round.

In 1897-98, Linlithgowshire teams had victories in the first round of the Qualifying Cup. Bathgate 8-1 against Vale of Leithen, Broxburn Shamrock 3-2 over Selkirk, and Bo'ness had a 4-1 victory away at Mossend, also playing in the town that day were Armadale Volunteers, who went down 4-0 to West Calder.

Struggling Shamrock scratched against Bo'ness, as senior football in Broxburn was on its last legs once again. Bathgate also went into the next round without kicking a ball as Trinity also scratched.

West Calder travelled to Penicuik, and with the game tied at 3-3, the West Calder keeper accidentally damaged the goalposts, and the visitors refused to wait until the goalposts were repaired, and the tie was awarded to Penicuik. The following round saw Bo'ness defeat Penicuik 1-0, while Bathgate received a bye. With both teams reaching the fourth round, automatic entry into the Scottish Cup was guaranteed, which was just as well as both fell heavily - Bathgate travelling to Loanhead and going down 7-0 to Polton Vale, while Bo'ness entertained near neighbours East Stirlingshire and were defeated 6-2.

Once again the Scottish Cup adventure was short lived when both Bathgate and Bo'ness failed at the first hurdle. First up was Bathgate against Cartvale at Boghead, within a few minutes of the start, Bathgate's Baillie opened the scoring. There were no more goals for the remainder of the half, as poor finishing prevented Cartvale from at the very least being on equal terms. The second half however, Cartvale equalised only for Bathgate to regain the lead. It seemed as if there would be no more scoring in the match as Bathgate sat back on their lead, but Cartvale's forwards had other ideas and caught the home defence napping in a five minute spell near the end, scored three goals and ultimately snatched victory by 4-2. This could have been a blessing in disguise as a couple of weeks later on the 22nd January, Cartvale were hammered 12-0 against Rangers at Ibrox.

A crowd of around 2000 gathered to see Bo'ness take on Queens Park, and the Glasgow amateurs were taking nothing for granted and fielded a very strong side. A plucky Bo'ness side had no answer to the well organised visitors, and three goals in each half saw Queen's cruise into the next round.

THE BIGGER PICTURE

Kilmarnock beat Dundee 3-2, in the second semi final, but it took three attempts for Rangers to defeat Third Lanark (1-1, 2-2, 2-0), the final being played at Hampden ending in a 2-0 win for Rangers.

Season 1898-99 and County teams continued to struggle against professionalism; Broxburn Shamrock had all but given up their bid to field a team and scratched to Vale of Leithen. This proved the final straw for the club and they were kicked out the competition for failing to play two qualifying rounds in successive seasons.

Bathgate went out to Penicuik 3-0 after 1-1 and 2-2 draws. Polton Vale disposed of Armadale Volunteers 4-1, Selkirk scratched to Bo'ness, while the shock of the round saw Mossend Swifts heavily defeated against neighbours West Calder by an 8-1 score line.

The second round saw both Bo'ness and West Calder progress into the next round, the former winning 3-0 against Adventurers, with Vale of Leithen scratching to the latter. The third round saw a 3-2 victory for Bo'ness over Polton Vale, while West Calder travelled to Clackmannan and recorded a fine 2-1 victory. Both teams were given byes in the fourth round which meant Scottish Cup qualification. The fifth round saw a 3-2 home win for Bo'ness against Forfar Athletic, while West Calder travelled to Falkirk, but went down 3-1 to East Stirlingshire. Eventually Bo'ness met their match in the quarter finals, going down 2-1 to Arbroath after a 2-2 draw.

The Scottish Cup first rounds saw the visit of First Division St. Bernards to Bo'ness. The *Edinburgh Evening Dispatch* reported that St. Bernards played poorly and it was just another example of the danger of treating opponents cheaply, and entering into a match confident of victory. The Saints will probably have a greater respect now for the Bo'ness men. Bo'ness with a strong wind advantage had taken a 3-1 half time lead. Saints were in for a shock if they thought they were going to have it all their own way, in fact it was only when the Bo'ness players began to tire in the last fifteen minutes that the visitors scored twice to force a replay.

The replay at Logie Green was watched by an attendance of around 3000, who witnessed an exciting end to end game. Even though there were numerous chances for both teams the first half ended goalless. The second half started in similar fashion but this time the net was found on six occasions. Like the first match, it was St. Bernard's fitness level that carried them through with a 4-2 victory. Bo'ness were by no means disgraced, and it was one of the better games the club had played during the season. The other first round ties saw West Calder make the long journey up north to take on Forfar Athletic, the visitors making it worthwhile with a 5-4 victory.

The second round saw West Calder on the road yet again, this time travelling west to take on Second Division hopefuls Port Glasgow Athletic,

47

but the home side proved too much for West Calder, as they went down by three goals to one.

THE BIGGER PICTURE

Port Glasgow Athletic were beaten 4-2 by Celtic, with Rangers setting up an Old Firm final, after defeating St. Mirren 2-1. In this the second Old Firm final, Celtic took the honours winning 2-0 at Hampden Park.

Like Broxburn the previous season, it was now Armadale's turn once again to lose senior football, as the Volunteers called it a day, even though they entered the Qualifying Cup, they scratched to Mossend Swifts.

Bo'ness had a good home win over Bathgate 5-1, while West Calder had an even better result defeating Vale of Leithen 7-1. The second round saw both "Cauder" sides travel over to Fife, with both coming home empty handed. Mossend were beaten 2-0 by Cowdenbeath, while West Calder fell to Raith Rovers 1-0. Bo'ness were the only club to make it through to the next round, but it took a couple of games against underdogs Selkirk, finally winning 4-0 after a 1-1 draw.

Bo'ness recorded a 5-2 victory over Hearts of Beath, which sent them into the all important fourth round. There was no further progress sadly, as they were seen off 3-1 by Raith Rovers after a 2-2- draw. Bo'ness were rewarded with a visit to Glasgow to take on cup holders Celtic, the following report was taken from *The Courier;*

The cup holders met Bo'ness before a fair attendance of spectators. Teams – Celtic, McArthur, Davidson and Turnbull; Russell, Marshall and Orr; Bell and Somers; Divers, McMahon and Campbell. Bo'ness – Baillie, McMillan and Torrance; Sharp Devine and Murphy, Fulton and Devine, Kerr Patterson and Grant. Referee – Mr Black, Forfar. The Celts kicked off against the wind and scored in three minutes from a scrimmage. For half an hour the game consisted of almost ceaseless fusillade on the visitor's goal, but scoring was not an easy task, so well did Baillie and his backs defend. Corners and free kicks in innumerable fell to the Celts, but the visitors always cleared, sometimes very luckily. Bo'ness occasionally made headway, chiefly through the cleverness of Patterson and Grant, and twice McArthur had to exert himself. But otherwise the game was

48

dreadfully one sided, the only thing which interested the spectators being the miraculous escapes of Baillie. Half time, Celtic 1 Bo'ness 0. The Celts, on resuming were soon back at Baillie, but again they found scoring no easy task. Even a free kick granted on the penalty line that was cleared, but then after every one of the forwards had shot and headed without success, he got his foot in and beat Ballie with a fast shot. This practically decided the game, and it forced Bo'ness to open out, with the result that McMahon, Bell and Somers added goals. As such heavy scoring the home team took matters easy, but just before the finish, Divers scored a seventh goal and a run up by the visitors ended in McArthur fisting a long shot through his own goal. Result Celtic 7 Bo'ness 1.

THE BIGGER PICTURE

The Old Firm fought out a 2-2 draw before Celtic ran out 4-0 winners in the replay, Queens Park defeated Hearts 2-1 in the other semi-final. Celtic went on to lift the trophy with a 4-3 victory at Ibrox.

Only four local teams entered the 1900-01 Qualifying Cup, in the first round only one game was played, which resulted in Mossend Swifts defeating Bathgate 3-0. The other two games resulted in walk overs in the favour of the County clubs, Bo'ness against Adventurers and West Calder against Polton Vale.

The second round saw another walk over this time in Mossend's favour over Vale of Leithen, West Calder went down 3-0 at home to Bo'ness. The third round saw another walk over for Bo'ness to Edinburgh University and a bye for Mossend which made certain of a Scottish Cup place. The fourth round saw both teams go out of the competition, Bo'ness losing 3-0 to East Stirlingshire after a 1-1 draw, and Mossend going out to Stenhousemuir 5-1 after two 2-2 draws.

The first round of the Scottish Cup resulted in hammerings for both clubs. Bo'ness travelled to Greenock to take on First Division Morton, Bo'ness were weakly represented owing to players injuries. This could clearly be seen all over the park as all departments in the Bo'ness team failed to deliver; they could certainly have done with their former goalkeeper Briddle, who was on duty with the Royal Scots in South Africa. His replacement Campbell had a busy day picking the ball out of the net on no fewer than ten occasions. After putting on a special train it must have been disheartening for the Bo'ness support to watch, not even being able to cheer a consolation goal; the final score stood Morton 10 Bo'ness 0.

The other tie played at Tyncastle, Heart of Midlothian proved too much for Mossend, although not quite as heavy as the Cappielow result, Swifts were sent out the cup by 7-0, having made things even more difficult by having a man sent off.

THE BIGGER PICTURE

Celtic defeated St. Mirren 1-0 in the first semi final, while the second was a capital clash between Heart of Midlothian and Hibernian. After a 1-1 draw, Hearts eased into the final with a 2-1 victory. The cup headed east as Hearts lifted the trophy at Ibrox with a 4-3 victory.

1901-02 season saw a new name enter the competition, East Benhar Rangers, coming from the small village of East Benhar to the North of Fauldhouse. Not much is known about the side, and this was the only time the club entered the Qualifying Cup, drawn at home, "Rangers" went out first time of asking 4-2 to Dykehead.

It took Bo'ness three games to dispose of Bathgate, 3-3, 1-1, 2-1. West Calder had a great result defeating Second Division Leith Athletic 3-0, the final tie of the round saw Polton Vale scratch to Mossend. All three sides failed in the second round, all going out to Fife sides. Bo'ness went down 3-1 to Cowdenbeath; Lochgelly defeated Mossend 2-1, with the heaviest defeat coming West Calder's way as they crashed 6-1 to Raith Rovers. Since the first season of the introduction of the Qualifying Cup, this was to be the first time any County club failed to enter the Scottish Cup proper.

THE BIGGER PICTURE

For the second successive season, Celtic and St. Mirren clashed in the semi finals, once again it was Celtic who came out on top, with a 3-2 win. The other part of the Old Firm met Hibernian, with Hibs securing a 2-0 victory.

The final was played at Celtic Park on the 26th April 1902, and once again the trophy was heading east, with Hibernian scoring the only goal of the game. This final is still talked about to this very day, mainly by fans of Hibernian's bitter rivals Heart of Midlothian, as this was Hibernian's last success in the National Competition.

Broxburn FC were back on the scene after an absence of nearly ten years and got off to a winning start away to Mossend Swifts, with a splendid 7-0 victory. Bo'ness defeated Adventurers 4-3, while Bathgate saw off West Calder 5-3. Bathgate and Bo'ness were drawn together in the second round, and after a 1-1 draw, Bathgate eased through 3-2. Selkirk then scratched to Broxburn.

After a protest in a game Broxburn lost 2-1 , the replay resulted in an 8-3 win over Bathgate. The fourth round saw Broxburn lose their away game to Stenhousemuir 2-1. The first round of the "Scottish", Broxburn were drawn away to Leith Athletic at Logie Green. On a hard, heavily sanded pitch, only one goal separated the sides at the interval, but the second half however was mainly dominated by the home side who ran out 4-1 winners.

THE BIGGER PICTURE

Central Combination league side Stenhousemuir were the surprise team to make the Scottish Cup semi finals, but Rangers proved too much for the "non-leaguers" with a 4-1 victory. Hearts secured their place in the final with a 1-0 win over Dundee after a 0-0 draw.

The final required three matches before the trophy went to Rangers, all matches were played at Celtic Park, the first a 1-1 draw, followed by a 0-0 draw before Rangers secured the trophy with a 2-0 win.

1903-04 season saw the amalgamation of West Calder and Mossend Swifts, forming a new club by the name of West Calder Swifts. Considering the size of the village, two senior clubs was way too much for the people to support. Swifts got off to the best possible start with a 7-0 win over Adventurers, Bo'ness put ten past Selkirk, with Bathgate winning 5-3 over the Black Watch, Broxburn FC received a bye. The four were drawn together in the second round, and once again Bathgate and Broxburn were drawn together, and again the match was decided after a protest, with

Bathgate coming out on top on this occasion, with a 2-1 victory after an earlier 3-2 defeat, Swifts had a tight 2-1 home win over Bo'ness.

The third round paired up both clubs, where Swifts travelled to Bathgate to record a fine 3-1 victory. The fourth round saw another protested match, before Swifts eventually overcame Hearts of Beath 5-3. A 2-0 defeat after a 1-1 draw against Arbroath ended Swifts Qualifying Cup run, but it was enough to see them into the Scottish Cup proper. A first round visit into Edinburgh for Swifts to take on Second Division St. Bernards was the outcome, with a large crowd travelling from West Calder to cheer on their team. Swifts led 1-0 at half-time and should have doubled their lead just after the interval, when they were awarded a penalty kick, but the kick went wide of the post. This was to prove a costly mistake as St. Bernards equalised late in the game. With the draw being made for the next round, a home tie against Celtic added an additional incentive for both teams. A crowd of around 2,000 gathered and witnessed a thrilling end to the end game, with six goals being shared, but Swifts would have felt hard done by as they threw away a 3-1 lead in the dying minutes. The second replay took place at Mill Park Bathgate, again in front of an attendance of around 2,000. St. Bernards wining 2-0, both goals coming in the second half, and West Calder seemed to be completely disorganised, by having to act more defensively rather than playing their usual aggressive game.

THE BIGGER PICTURE

Celtic defeated First division champions Third Lanark 2-1, while Rangers saw off Morton 3-0 to set up the third Old Firm Final, with Celtic taking the honours with a 3-2 victory at Hampden Park.

Back on the scene for 1904-05 season were Broxburn Shamrock, who had moved to a new ground in the Goschen area of the town. The Qualifying Cup saw Shamrock drawn away to Bathgate, where the home side came out on top with a 3-1 win. Bo'ness saw off Adventurers 5-2 after a 1-1 draw, while Broxburn FC went down 1-0 to Leith Athletic. West Calder Swifts received a bye into the next round.

It was Bo'ness' turn to play Second Division Leith Athletic, and once again the league side eased through, this time by a 2-0 score line. West Calder

Swifts also tumbled out to Second League team St. Bernards for the second year running, losing 3-1 after a 1-1 draw. Borders club Newcastleton scratched to Bathgate. Bathgate then received a bye in the third round followed by an away win over Kirkcaldy. After another bye, they finally went out in the quarter finals to Clyde 2-0.

The first round of the "Scottish" saw Bathgate entertain Arbroath in front of a large attendance at Mill Park. Arbroath won the toss and took advantage of the strong wind, but by the interval Arbroath had only a solitary goal for their efforts. The second half opened in rousing fashion, with Bathgate pressing immediately, with the wind now in Bathgate's favour and increasing in velocity, it was no surprise when Lynn equalised for Bathgate. Minutes later Arbroath defender Ferguson headed into his own goal amidst tremendous cheering from the home support. Both teams had further chances before the final whistle, but it was Bathgate who held on for a memorable victory.

The second round saw Bathgate make the long trip north to Pittodrie to take on Aberdeen. A special train of more than two hundred supporters left from sunny Bathgate. Just under four hours later, the train arrived at snow covered Aberdeen. A pitch inspection at 2.30pm resulted in the match getting the go-ahead. Bathgate won the toss and left Aberdeen to fight against the wind and snow, all the early pressure came from Bathgate, but after twenty minutes, the referee who appeared to be feeling the effects of the storm stopped the game and the players retired into the pavilion. The snow eased after a few minutes and play resumed. Shortly after McPhee opened the scoring for Bathgate, however with half time approaching the home side equalised as the snow began to fall heavier. The second half kicked off and as expected Aberdeen dominated proceedings, but could not find a way past Bathgate's plucky defence. With now blizzard conditions the referee, after consulting both club captains, had little choice other than to abandon the game twenty five minutes from time. The following week Bathgate once again made the long journey up north, there was no snow, but a strong wind which Aberdeen took full advantage of. By half time the match was finished as a contest with the home side scoring six goals without reply. As Aberdeen sat back on their lead, Bathgate managed to pull a goal back three minutes into the second half, but this proved little more than a consolation with the score remaining 6-1 at the final whistle.

A share of the 6,000 gate which amounted to £169, made the trip that little bit worthwhile.

THE BIGGER PICTURE

Celtic and Rangers met in the semi finals, which resulted in a 2-0 win for the Light Blues, and Third Lanark booked their place in the final with a 2-1 win over Airdrieonians. Third Lanark went on to lift the trophy for the second and final time, winning 3-1 after a 0-0 draw.

With the West Calder clubs joining forces back in 1903, due to the town struggling to support two senior sides, it was most surprising to find no fewer than three Broxburn sides entering the Qualifying Cup. Joining Broxburn FC and Broxburn Shamrock were junior side Broxburn Athletic, who decided to step up and join the senior ranks. Athletic fell at the first attempt though, going down 5-0 away to Bo'ness. Broxburn FC also stumbled out, going down to Leith Athletic 2-0 after a 1-1 draw. Shamrock the final side from the trio progressed into the next round defeating Adventurers 4-1 after a protested match, which the Irishmen had also won 3-2. West Calder Swifts went out quickly after losing 2-1 following a draw against Berwick Rangers, also out were Bathgate, with a 4-2 defeat against St. Bernards.

Bo'ness revenged Swifts last round defeat against Berwick Rangers by beating the Englishmen 2-1. Shamrocks were 7-0 winners over Selkirk. Both remaining West Lothian sides then met in the third round, with Bo'ness coming out on top 3-0. Having already qualified for the Scottish Cup proper, Bo'ness went out 3-1 to Hamilton Academicals in the fourth round.
Bo'ness travelled to Arbroath and recorded a fine 4-1 victory, two goals in either half, the first coming in under five minutes. This set Bo'ness onto a victory, but the win was chiefly down to excellent defending from the Bo'ness rearguard, with goalkeeper, Wemyss in great form.

The second round draw once again paired Bo'ness with Glasgow giants Celtic at Celtic Park. The Bo'ness club had come a long way since their last visit to the east end of Glasgow back in 1900. With some recent singings from teams such as Airdrieonians, Hibs, Hearts and Rangers, as well as a few players from south of the border, a repeat of the 7-1 hammering was never likely to be on the cards. The game kicked off at 3.15pm after a crowd of 5,000 had gathered, 800 of whom had travelled from Bo'ness to lend their support. The first half belonged to Celtic, where Bo'ness was quite simply overwhelmed, and the few chances they did muster gave only a glimpse of their true form. By the time the whistle blew for the interval, Celtic were leading 3-0, and like in the previous round, they had the keeper Wemyss to thank for keeping the score line respectable. The second half however was a different story, with Bo'ness doing all the early running and the large Bo'ness support getting right behind their team. Celtic did eventually come into the game, and the second half was more evenly matched. Both teams had chances but there was to be no more scoring and the match finished 3-0 to Celtic.

THE BIGGER PICTURE

Heart of Midlothian made another final appearance defeating Port Glasgow Athletic 2-0, but it took three matches to decide their opponents, before Third Lanark eventually saw off St. Mirren (1-1, 0-0, 1-0). The trophy once again headed east where Hearts recorded a 1-0 win.

Season 1906-07 saw seven teams enter the Qualifying Cup, but all failed to reach the important fourth round for the Scottish Cup qualification. New to the scene was Winchburgh side West Lothian Albion. The newcomers produced a surprise 4-1 win away to West Calder Swifts. Broxburn Athletic only into their second senior season also caused an upset with a 3-2 victory over Bo'ness after a 0-0 draw. Edinburgh sides Leith Athletic and St. Bernards saw off Broxburn pair Broxburn FC and Shamrock respectively, and finally Bathgate hammered Berwick Rangers 5-1 at Mill Park. Once again the Edinburgh teams saw off our county clubs, St. Bernards putting five past Broxburn Athletic without reply, while Leith Athletic travelled to Winchburgh to record a 2-0 win. Bathgate entertained the soldiers from the Royal Garrison artillery winning 2-0, finally going down to Cowdenbeath 1-0 after 2-2 and 1-1 draws.

THE BIGGER PICTURE

Hibernian and Hearts were drawn apart in the semi finals, with Hearts defeating Queens Park 1-0, but there was to be no Edinburgh final as Hibernian lost out to Celtic 3-0 after two 0-0 draws. The following week, 20th April, Celtic lifted the cup with the same score line.

Back on the scene after a long absence was Uphall. Along with the Broxburn trio and Albion from Winchburgh, it's difficult to imagine five teams from the same proximity all fighting out for Scottish Cup glory. At least two of the clubs would make the second round, as four were drawn together. Broxburn Athletic knocked out Broxburn FC 1-0 after a 1-1 draw, and it took Uphall two matches to overcome Shamrock with a 3-2 victory after a 0-0 draw. For the second year running, Leith Athletic won 2-0 at Winchburgh. Bo'ness also recorded a 2-0 win over Bathgate after a 1-1 draw. West Calder Swifts received a bye.

Only Broxburn Athletic failed in the second round, going out narrowly to Second Division club St. Bernards 1-0. Fellow league strugglers Cowdenbeath lost out to Bo'ness 2-0 after a 0-0 draw, while West Calder Swifts had a fine 4-1 away win at Stenhousemuir. Finally, Uphall saw off Clackmannan 2-1 after a 3-3 draw. West Calder Swifts made a lengthy trip to Elgin before going down 2-1, a win for Bo'ness against Alloa Athletic 2-1 and a 3-0 victory for Uphall over Aberdeen University saw both clubs reaching the all important fourth round. Bo'ness had a good 3-1 win over Scottish League side Ayr Parkhouse after a 1-1 draw, and Uphall tumbled out at Dumfries 3-1, with the southern side repeating the feat in the fifth round to put an end to Bo'ness hopes.

Uphall travelled to Ayrshire, where hosts Galston recorded an easy 6-0 victory, leading 4-0 at half time, and the game was finished as a contest. Bo'ness were drawn away to Partick Thistle. Prior to the game a heavy rain and hail fell, which made underfoot conditions difficult. This also affected the crowd, as barely 1,000 spectators were present. Struggling Bo'ness lost two goals either half, going down 4-0.

THE BIGGER PICTURE

Aberdeen lost out to Celtic 1-0, while St. Mirren saw off Kilmarnock 2-0 after a 0-0 draw. Goals were plentiful in the final, with Celtic recording a 5-1 win.

Hardly surprising then, that there was no Broxburn Shamrock for the start of the 1908-09 campaign, many in Broxburn argued that even two clubs was too much for the town, never mind three! Nevertheless, both remaining clubs from the town got off to great starts, Athletic had a 2-0 home win over Bo'ness, Broxburn FC scoring three without reply against Uphall.

Edinburgh's Second Division sides, St. Bernards and Leith Athletic, saw off West Lothian Albion and Bathgate respectively, West Calder Swifts received a bye. Second round saw Broxburn FC defeat Division Two high flyers Raith Rovers 1-0 at Broxburn. West Calder Swifts had a close 2-1 home win over Broxburn Athletic, but enough to see them progress into the third round. A bye for Broxburn FC saw them enter the Scottish Cup proper for the first time since 1902-03 season. West Calder Swifts joined them with a 2-1 victory over Dunfermline Athletic. West Calder Swifts and Elgin City met for the second successive season, Swifts gaining revenge with a 2-1 home win. Broxburn FC went down to Leith Athletic 3-1 after a 2-2 draw. A fifth round defeat to Brechin City 2-0 after a 0-0 draw ended Swifts Qualifying Cup hopes.

Five games were needed between Broxburn FC and Beith, to decide their Scottish Cup first round tie. With Broxburn drawn at home, this was the first Scottish cup match in the town for several years, which in turn produced a great deal of local interest. Over a thousand spectators witnessed a hugely disappointing game, with the match finishing 1-1. In the replay the following week at Beith, again the clubs could not be separated, in what was described as another drab encounter. The clubs met on the 3rd February at Ibrox and even after extra time the result stood at 1-1. The following night and once again at Ibrox Park, another two hours passed, but both teams were still on level pegging with another 1-1 draw. The next day, 5th February- the day before the next round games, Beith eventually won through with a 4-2 victory at Love Street. Not surprising Beith eventually went down 3-0 to St. Mirren. In the other tie, West Calder

Swifts entertained Partick Thistle at Burngrange Park. Although Thistle were the more organised side, Swifts made up for it in their fighting manner, and thoroughly deserved another chance by holding the First Division side to a goalless draw. Partick Thistle at that time did not seem to have a suitable venue for the replay, so Swifts tried to get the replay at Burngrange. Thistle refused and appealed to the Association, and as a result it was decided that the game should take place at Shawfield. When the tie was due to be played, Swifts failed to turn up, which resulted in Thistle going through to the next round.

THE BIGGER PICTURE

There were no winners of the 1908-09 Scottish Cup. Semi-final victories for Celtic 2-0 over Clyde after a 0-0 draw and a 1-0 win for Rangers over Falkirk brought about another Old Firm derby. After a 2-2 draw on 10th April, both clubs met the following week, and again the match ended in a draw, 1-1. Although the game throughout its early years had seen its fair share of crowd trouble, what was about to be witnessed after the second drawn match was to be the first major outbreak of hooliganism in Scotland. Some spectators believed that extra time would take place, although both teams understood that was not to be the case. As the teams left the field, sections of the crowd fought with police and among themselves. The supporters then went on the rampage as they ripped out the goalposts, tore down wooden railings to make fires, and the pay boxes around Hampden were also badly damaged by fire. The next day Celtic and Rangers issued a joint statement saying that the final should be abandoned without a result because of the regrettable occurrences. Although the Scottish FA suggested a third match outside the city, both clubs stuck to their decision and the trophy and medals were withheld.

After a year out, Broxburn Shamrock made a surprise return in a home tie against Leith Athletic (a team who finished top of the Second Division that season), who proved too much for Shamrock with a 5-0 victory. Broxburn Athletic also went down to Edinburgh opposition, St. Bernards 3-1. The third team from the town Broxburn FC progressed with a bye, and elsewhere saw victories for Bathgate 3-0 over West Lothian Albion.

Bo'ness also put three by West Calder Swifts, and Uphall's short existence ceased once again.

Second round wins for Bathgate 2-1 over East Stirlingshire, and Bo'ness 2-1 winners over Stenhousemuir (after protest) saw them both progress into the next round. Broxburn however, were not so lucky falling 2-1 at home to East Fife.

Both Bathgate and Bo'ness were given byes in to the all important fourth round, both playing Scottish League sides. Bathgate travelled to Glasgow and defeated First Division side Partick Thistle 2-1, but Bo'ness failed at home to Dumbarton 1-0. A quarter final win over Kirkcaldy 3-1 after a1-1 draw, followed by a single goal win over Dumbarton, and Bathgate had booked their place in the Qualifying Cup final, a first time for a County club. The final was played at Easter Road in front of 9,000 spectators, who saw Bathgate lose 4-0 to Leith Athletic.

In the first round of the "Scottish", Bo'ness were drawn away against Aberdeen. With the Bo'ness club already en-route, the Pittodrie pitch was deemed unplayable covered by snow and frost. The teams decided to play a friendly in order to recoup some of the Bo'ness expenses. However, with Aberdeen playing a reserve team and the players taking no risks, the game was little more than a training session, and the match ended in a 2-2 draw. The game was eventually played a fortnight later, and First Division Aberdeen proved too much for Bo'ness, within fifteen minutes they were 2-0 up. Although Aberdeen took their foot off the pedal they still dominated proceedings, but failed to add to the score before the interval. Into the second half and Bo'ness created a few chances, but there was only going to be one winner, as Aberdeen tied up the game with a third goal. The only Scottish Cup tie played in the County was the Bathgate v Heart of Midlothian at Mill Park, and the headline in the *Courier* read;

BATHGATE'S FINE DISPLAY FIRST HALF, HEARTS TOP DOG SECOND PORTION AND WIN EASILY

A crowd of over 4,000 gathered at Mill Park witnessed a fine game, played in treacherous conditions amidst snow and ice. Bathgate players adapted to the surface quicker than the Edinburgh men, and for the first thirty minutes had the bulk of play and caused the visitors defence problems before Hearts scored through Colombo. Before half time, Bathgate had a strong penalty appeal turned down when Law was shoved off the ball in the box by Walker. Minutes later Tennant almost equalised for the home side as the half time whistle sounded, Bathgate at this stage were certainly worth a share of the spoils.

On resuming, Bathgate were first on the attack, but a good clearance set up Hearts for a second goal. Hearts now playing with confidence, added a further two goals, before sitting back and seeing out the remainder of the match, the final score of 4-0 certainly flattered the Tynecastle club.

THE BIGGER PICTURE

Clyde defeated Celtic 3-1 in the first semi-final, after a previous 2-0 win over Rangers, making Clyde hot favourites to lift the trophy. Clyde's opponents were eventually decided when Dundee hit the only goal of the game against Hibernian, at the third attempt, previous matches ending 0-0. The final turned out to be another marathon, with the first game ending 2-2, Clyde throwing away a 2-0 lead in the last five minutes, the replayed match ended goal-less, Clyde eventually paid the price losing by 2-1. This to date is Dundee's only cup win.

Season 1910-11 saw the welcome return of Armadale back into senior football, and also entry of the Qualifying Cup after a lapse of over ten years. After 1-1 and 2-2 draws, Armadale eventually saw off Broxburn Shamrock 5-0 at Bathgate's Mill Park. It also took three games to decide the outcome between near neighbours West Lothian Albion and Broxburn FC, with the latter winning 4-1 after 1-1- and 0-0 draws. Once again the Edinburgh pair Leith Athletic and St. Bernards proved too strong for Bathgate and Broxburn Athletic respectively. The Bathgate match took four games to decide due to draws and protests, the final game of the round involving County clubs. Bo'ness saw off West Calder Swifts 3-0.

Only Bo'ness got past the second round with an easy 5-0 defeat of Vale of Leithen. Armadale lost 2-0 to Leith Athletic and a 3-1 home defeat ended Broxburn FC hopes against Peebles Rovers. Bo'ness did what Broxburn FC couldn't, defeating Peebles Rovers 2-1 after a protest. A defeat away to

Lochgelly United 1-0 made little difference for the coastal side as they marched into the first round of the Scottish Cup.

Bo'ness visited Broomfield Park to take on Airdrieonians. With the home side having three players sidelined, it was felt Bo'ness may be in with a chance of producing a shock over the first leaguers. Airdrieonians however did not make the mistake of under-estimating the abilities of Bo'ness, and in less than two minutes they took the lead through Combe; the same player added another before half time. Both teams had chances in the second half, but Airdrieonians thoroughly deserved their victory.

Bathgate F.C. © West Lothian Local History Library

THE BIGGER PICTURE

Hamilton Academicals defeated last year's winners Dundee 3-2 to set up a final appearance with Celtic, who had beaten Aberdeen with the only goal of the game. A replay was needed after a 0-0 draw, which Celtic won 2-0.

Qualifying Cup 1911-12 season, and once again Edinburgh sides St. Bernards and Leith Athletic were a thorn in the West Lothian club's sides, knocking out Broxburn Shamrock and Broxburn FC respectively.

Broxburn Athletic went down 5-0 to West Calder Swifts, but due to a professional irregularity, the match was replayed and finished 0-0. The third game which saw Athletic leading 1-0 did not finish due to a pitch invasion, but the Broxburn side were awarded the tie. Bo'ness surprisingly went down 6-1 at home to Bathgate, with Armadale recording a 4-1 win over West Lothian Albion. Bathgate continued their good work, knocking out St. Bernards 3-1 after a 1-1 draw, and Broxburn Athletic defeated Peebles Rovers 1-0, but not before protesting the first match which they had lost 2-0. The final match of the round saw Armadale win 10-0 at home against Duns, who had sold ground advantage for £10. The Borders side then appeared at Armadale with only nine men, with the 'Dale lending them two players to apparently even up the numbers!

The third round saw Broxburn Athletic beat Gala Fairydean 2-1; Bathgate and Armadale met at Mill Park where the visitors came away with a 2-1 victory. East Stirlingshire ended Armadale's run with a 2-0 victory after three drawn games. Broxburn Athletics' run also came to an end going down 2-1 at home to Leith Athletic, but their places in the Scottish Cup were secure.

This was Broxburn Athletics' first taste of the national competition, and they turned on one of their best performances in a long time in one of the most one sided matches ever to be witnessed at Albion Park. The 6-0 victory even surprised Athletics 400 or so support, who had gathered to watch a Beith side who a couple of years earlier knocked Broxburn FC out of the competition in that five match marathon, but three goals either half ensured Athletic of a easy victory.

In the other cup game, Armadale entertained Peterhead in what was their first Scottish Cup tie in over twenty years, on a very hard Volunteer Park. The game kicked off in wintry conditions, and with half time approaching, Armadale eventually took the lead following a scrimmage in the goalmouth. It was a wonder the referee allowed the goal to stand, as Armadale players were falling over one another, the ball being handled on more than one occasion. Peterhead levelled, but with twelve minutes remaining, Menzies scored the winner for the Armadale and saved the West Lothian men a long trip up north.

The second round however put paid to that as Armadale were drawn against Aberdeen. Even though the 'Dale came out the hat first, they gave up home advantage for £40, as this would help pay off debts that had mounted up over the past year. The match was won by Aberdeen 3-0, the first goal coming within a couple of minutes. Good defending by Armadale kept the score down, but they had their work cut out in the second half when Rankin got his marching orders, in what was a rough second half.

Broxburn Athletic also gave up home advantage in a hope of making some extra cash, much to the disgust of their support. Athletic travelled though to Glasgow to take on Third Lanark in front of an estimated 2,500 fans. Thirds ran out easy winners 6-1, Raitt scoring a second half hat-trick.

THE BIGGER PICTURE

Celtic progressed into the final with a 3-0 win over Heart of Midlothian, with Clyde joining them, beating Third Lanark 3-1. Celtic retained the trophy with a 2-0 win.

Season 1912-13 saw a big change for the County. First up saw Broxburn FC and Broxburn Athletic join forces to form Broxburn United. Also finishing up were Winchburgh side West Lothian Albion, as the past couple of seasons had been a struggle for the club mainly due to the close proximity of Broxburn. Albion did enter the Qualifying Cup but scratched to Bathgate. The "new" Broxburn side got off to the best possible start with a 2-0 home win over Bo'ness.

Armadale saw off Musselburgh 3-1 at home, while West Calder Swifts hammered Black Watch 8-1 away from home. Broxburn Shamrock failed miserably away to Leith Athletic going down 6-0. Only Broxburn United managed to get by the second round defeating West Calder Swifts 1-0, Bathgate lost 2-1 to St. Bernards at Mill Park. Finally Armadale travelled down to Galashiels going out of the competition 1-0 to Gala Fairydean. A bye in the third round for Broxburn United secured United's first Scottish Cup appearance, a narrow 1-0 home defeat in the fourth round by Second Division side Dundee Hibernian didn't seem too significant as all eyes were now on the Scottish Cup.

The draw was made, which paired them against First Division strugglers Raith Rovers at the Sports Park. Rovers did however succeed in buying over home advantage, and United officials were probably influenced by the fact that their side was not playing well enough to warrant the belief they would stand a chance at home. Furthermore, the extra money would be more useful in attracting better players to the club. At the end of the day the right choice had been made, as United went down 5-0.

THE BIGGER PICTURE

As it turned out Broxburn United's conquerors Raith Rovers went on a run, before ending up beaten finalists. The Kirkcaldy side defeated Clyde 1-0 after a replay, both games played at Tynecastle. The other semi-final saw Falkirk overcome Heart of Midlothian 1-0 at Ibrox. Falkirk went on to lift the trophy for the first time with a 2-0 victory at Celtic Park.

Once again the Edinburgh pair Leith Athletic and St. Bernards did the damage against West Lothian sides, knocking out Broxburn Shamrock and Armadale respectively, although it took a replay on both occasions. Bathgate progressed with a 3-2 away win at Bo'ness while West Calder Swifts scratched to Leith Amateurs. Broxburn United received a bye into the next round and then recorded a 1-0 win over Bathgate at Mill Park. Broxburn United then travelled over the border and came home with a 3-0 win over Berwick Rangers, another away tie this time to Kirkcaldy ended United's run with a 1-0 defeat.

Broxburn United received a bye in the first round of the Scottish Cup, which lead the way to a home tie against Dumfries. A crowd of around 1,500 gathered to see United march into the next round, with an easy victory in a match the Broxburn side totally dominated. They struggled to find the net however, and by the interval were leading by only a single goal. The second half was a different story when United added a further four goals. Late on when the home side seemed to slacken off, Dumfries grabbed a consolation; final score Broxburn United 5 Dumfries 1.

The third round saw the visit of First Division Motherwell to the Sports Park, a tempting offer of £120 was turned down by the Broxburn officials to have the tie switched to Fir Park, much to the delight of the Broxburn support. On a fine Saturday afternoon, the game took place in front of a record crowd of around 5,000 - 2,000 of whom travelled from the Lanarkshire town. Motherwell adapted to the game quickly and within a minute struck the crossbar. A few minutes later Broxburn had a golden chance to open the scoring as Kelly was clean through on goal, but his final shot let him down.

With twelve minutes on the clock, Motherwell opened the scoring through Whitehead after a slip-up by Henderson. Minutes later and Broxburn were 2-0 down, Hillhouse scoring with an over-head kick. Both teams had chances to score, with Motherwell quite happy to soak up any Broxburn pressure and clear their lines. This at times resulted in the ball leaving the field, much to the disgust of the home support. The game finished with Broxburn pressing hard, but there was to be no more scoring as the game ended 2-0 to the visitors.

Armadale F.C. 1914 © West Lothian Local History Library

THE BIGGER PICTURE

What was to be the last cup final before the Great War, Celtic earned their place with a 2-0 win over Third Lanark. Hibernian joined them by beating St. Mirren at Tynecastle 3-1. Celtic went on to lift the trophy for the ninth time with a 4-1 win, after a 0-0 draw.

The First World War temporarily ended the Scottish Cup competition, but the Scottish Qualifying Cup carried on as per usual. For Broxburn Shamrock and West Calder Swifts, this was to spell the end for both clubs in senior football. Shamrock went down 4-1 at home to Bo'ness, with Swifts also at home losing 3-1 to Armadale. Broxburn United needed a replay to see off Leith Amateurs, United eventually winning 3-1, Leith Athletic knocked out Bathgate with the same score line.

The second round and Armadale didn't seem to have the same problems as Bathgate in the previous round as they recorded a 2-0 victory over Leith Athletic. Bo'ness' journey down to the borders was all in vain as Gala Fairydean shocked the Blues with a 2-1 victory, Vale of Leithen scratched to Broxburn United. Broxburn defeated Gala Fairydean 3-0, while Armadale received a bye into the fourth round, but that's as far as they got in the competition. Broxburn lost 4-0 to St. Bernards after a 0-0 draw, while Armadale crashed out 3-0 to Galston.

Like the Scottish Cup, the Qualifying Cup was also put on hold till 1919-20 season, due to the war. When the competition finally got underway, the County was reduced to only four senior teams; Armadale, Bathgate, Bo'ness and Broxburn United. There was to be a first round defeat for United as Armadale won through 2-1 after a 1-1 draw. Bathgate defeated St. Bernards by the only goal of the game, while Bo'ness crushed Leith Amateurs 7-0 at Newtown.

The second round saw Armadale dispose of Peebles Rovers 6-2, and Bo'ness recorded a 1-0 win against Gala Fairydean, & Bathgate received a bye into the third round. Bathgate then knocked out Bo'ness 2-0 at home, and it was Armadale's turn for a bye, both reaching the fourth round and once again byes were the order of the day for both clubs. Bathgate beat fellow Central League side St. Johnstone 4-1, while Armadale travelled north to take on Inverness Caledonian, and booked a place in the quarter finals with a 1-0 win. That's as far as the 'Dale managed however, going down 2-1 to Cowdenbeath. Bathgate on the other hand were going great guns, hammering Arbroath 6-1 at Mill Park. A semi final win over Vale of Leven 1-0 set up another final appearance in the competition for the Bathgate club, this time Cowdenbeath were to be their opponents.

With all due respect to the West Lothian clubs, the Qualifying Cup was realistically the only chance provincial clubs would have of landing a national trophy, and as it turned out, Bathgate did just that. On the 27th December 1919 in front of 6,000 fans at Ibrox, Bathgate came away with a 2-0 victory. A special train for Bathgate's support started at Drumshoreland station in Broxburn, picking up along the way in Uphall, Livingston, Bathgate, Armadale and West Craigs. As was expected support came from all round the county, a number of motor "shara-bangs" were also chartered to run through to Ibrox. Both eastern clubs were disappointed with the SFA's decision to hold the final at Ibrox rather than the more obvious choice of Edinburgh, which would have certainly attracted a far greater attendance. The weather greatly affected the gate as heavy rain and sleet fell before kick-off, as supporters crammed into the two enclosures in the ground seeking shelter.

Bathgate players were first out on the pitch, greeted by a hearty reception. The line up was as follows; *Wilkinson, Hay, Black, Garrett, Godfrey, McArthur, Early, Brogan, Anderson, Campbell and Smith.* Bathgate kicked off, playing against the strong wind and rain, but despite their handicap the Mill Park side stuck tenaciously to their task and had quite an equal share of the game. After twenty six minutes Brogan hit a powerful drive that completely beat McKinlay to put Bathgate one ahead. Ten minutes later, an excellent individual effort from Anderson doubled their lead. After Bathgate's second goal, Cowdenbeath did most of the pressing, but the Bathgate rear guard stood firm, with Wilkinson at his usual best in goal. There was to be no more scoring, and the cup was heading back to Bathgate, final result stood Cowdenbeath 0 Bathgate 2.

News of the result soon filtered back to the town, and many people with only a passing interest gave free and open expression of delight. At the Cinema House, the result was thrown on the screen at the children's matinee and was greeted with uproarious applause by the young enthusiasts.

By the time the special train arrived back at Bathgate at 8.00pm, a huge crowd had gathered at the station. Both sides of the Whitburn Road and Engine Street were lined with people, both male and female, anxious to get a view of the football trophy. No sooner had the players made their exit from the station, than they were surrounded by a wildly excited crowd who showered congratulations on every member of the team. Captain Godfrey was quickly "chaired" and with the cup held aloft, the triumphal march commenced. The scene as witnessed in Engine Street, had seldom been seen in Bathgate. The whole street was filled with a huge slow moving mass of people, and the cheering was kept up continuously. For the sheer good nature and spontaneous enthusiasm, it would have been difficult to beat.

Less than a month after Bathgate's Qualifying Cup triumph, the team visited Edinburgh to take on St. Bernards in the Scottish Cup. Only a couple of changes had been made from the cup winning side. A crowd of between 6,000 and 7,000 gathered, many travelling from Bathgate, but it was not to be Bathgate's day, even though the visitors had their fair share of the play, they failed to get past a solid St. Bernards defence. On the other hand, the home team took their chances scoring in each half, final result St. Bernards 2 Bathgate 0.

With Broxburn receiving a bye into the second round, the only other tie to take place was at Armadale, where they played hosts to First Division Clyde. A large crowd was anticipated and measures were put in place to provide suitable accommodation for the support, and the banking around the ground was raised considerably. As it turned out, around 5,000 spectators attended; also in attendance were the Armadale Public Band, who entertained the large crowd before kick-off.

Armadale won the toss and set their opponents to face the incline. Armadale were quick off the mark and soon had the Glasgow side under pressure, the visitors could find little headway and seldom bothered the home goal. Worse was to follow for the visitors, when centre forward Allan had to retire due to a knee injury just before half time. The second half was mainly all Armadale as Clyde struggled with ten men. It looked as if they had managed to secure a replay, only for Armadale's Willie Fleming to slide home the only goal of the game with ten minutes remaining, sending the home support wild with excitement. Clyde made a desperate effort to save the situation, but the Armadale defence remained firm and retired worthy winners.

Armadale's reward for the defeat of First Division Clyde was another home tie, which saw another First Division side, Hibernian travel out from Edinburgh. Once again records were broken as the Volunteer ground burst at the seams as seven thousand supporters crammed in to witness the second round clash. Two thousand had journeyed from Edinburgh, a few of whom had other intentions than just watching the football match, as quite a number of Armadale men had their pockets "picked" during the match.

The game got underway with Armadale kicking up hill, as the game swung from end to end, with both teams looking to break the deadlock. In the tenth minute, a breakaway by Smith sent a perfect cross over to Prentice, who in turn found the back of the net, to an almighty cheer from around the ground. The remainder of the match produced several chances, mainly from Hibernian, but they found Armadale keeper Robb in excellent form. During the final five minutes of the game, Armadale were forced to play with ten men through the injury of Kiernan, but the home side survived and nearly added a second in the last minute. At the end of the day, Armadale once again thoroughly deserved their win. Armadale 1 Hibernian 0.

The other second round tie was played at the Sports Park, where Broxburn United entertained Queen of the South in front of around 2,500 spectators, which included a small band of supporters from Dumfries. United had the bulk of the play, the home keeper didn't have a save to make until early into the second half. This in turn seemed to have spurred the home team on, and after a good spell of pressure, Chambers headed home the only goal of the game. Queen's battled bravely but the score remained 1-0 for the home side.

Broxburn United were in the money as they were paired with Glasgow Rangers at Ibrox for their third round tie, with the following report being taken from *The West Lothian Courier;*

BROXBURN UNITED GO DOWN BEFORE RANGERS
WEAKENED TEAM PUT UP A GOOD FIGHT

Rangers: Lock, Manderson, Gordon, Bowie, Dixon, Walls, Archibald, Muirhead, Cunningham, Cairns, and Patterson.

Broxburn United: Stirling, McColl, McLean, Drennan, Chambers, O'Brian, Kidd, Dick, Sutherland, McGibbons, and Currie.

Referee: Mr J B Stevenson, Motherwell.

Close on 20,000 persons witnessed the kick off. Broxburn were without the services of Barnes, their capable halfback, who was unable to play on account of injuries, Sutherland of Pumpherston took up the position at centre. Rangers lost the toss and came away strongly, Muirhead placing nicely to Cunningham, who missed a fair chance. Patterson however, was fairly on the mark soon after, a shot from the left-winger testing Stirling, who succeeded in holding and clearing. Cunningham was again unlucky with a nice pass from Patterson. The Rangers were having all of the play, and only occasionally did the visitors get over the half way line. McGibbons being conspicuous in these efforts and Manderson clearing cleverly on behalf of the home side. Patterson continued to catch the eye in several good efforts by him were successfully dealt with by Stirling. Muirhead had a nice run, which brought a score, that player heading through after a save by Stirling. This occurred after 20 minutes of play. Broxburn showed plenty of pluck in getting within range, Sutherland twice tested the Rangers keeper, and Kidd was unlucky to be pulled up for offside when in a prominent position. Rangers however, were masters and Cunningham from a pass by Cairns secured a second goal, the ball glancing from the post into the net. Half time, Rangers 2 Broxburn Utd 0.

Mid-field play ruled after the assumption, Archibald and Cairns were the first to get away from the Rangers, and the former rounding McLean, set in a hard shot, the ball striking the outside of the net. Broxburn had a look in through Curie who failed with a weak shot. The Rangers came back and Stirling held a hard ball from Bowie, then Archibald sent over with the keeper well out of goal. Just on time, penalty was awarded to Rangers and Dixon scored;

Result: Rangers 3 Broxburn United 0

Broxburn United 1924 © Mr Stewart McLean

By reason of their recent performances in the Scottish Cup, Armadale had jumped into unprecedented prominence in the football world. In recent weeks within the national press, they were the most talked about provincial team in Scotland. With First Division opposition for the third time to visit Volunteer Park, speculation was rife throughout the County as to the fate of Ayr United, but as a whole, the Ayrshire men were going into the game as clear favourites.

For around two hours before kick-off, the vicinity of Armadale Cross presented an unusually lively scene as a huge fleet of motor vehicles of every description from buses to cars each carrying well over their legal requirements had gathered. The local bus service between Armadale and Bathgate could only cope with a small percentage of supporters, with many of the crowd walking from the outlying districts. The arrival of a special train from Ayr with around 1,000 supporters added to the density of the crowd and it was soon evident that all previous records for Volunteer Park were about to be broken. By the time the players appeared on the park, 8,000 spectators were squashed into the ground. Armadale made two changes to the team that knocked out Hibernian, McCaig and Poole replacing Harris and Prentice, the following team lined up; *Robb, Dick,*

Kiernan, McCaig, Kirkbride, Gardener, Speirs, Sullivan, Poole, Fleming and Smith.

An evenly matched first half saw the game swing from end to end without either of the keepers having a great deal to do. Both defences stood firm, with Armadale having the best of the chances and should really have been at least one goal ahead at the interval. On the hour mark however, Armadale eventually took the lead, with great work from Poole down the right side, crossing the ball into the box which found Smith, who in turn neatly guided it into the net. Ayr had a spell after this goal, but Robb in goal was in outstanding form, and as time ticked away it looked as if the keeper was going to have another clean sheet, only for disaster to strike when an Ayr corner was floated into the box. There didn't seem to be any immediate danger as Armadale's Dick handled the ball, and the referee awarded a penalty, which Ayr gratefully accepted and tied the score. Both teams had chances to win the tie, but the score remained Armadale 1 Ayr United 1.

The following week on the 28th February, Armadale visited Somerset Park for the replay. The press had the match down for an easy Ayr win, in fact one paper *The Glasgow News* went another step further by advertising the following week's fixtures which included Ayr Utd v Kilmarnock! The Armadale team were accompanied by a large local support, and like Bathgate in the Qualifying Cup Final, support was on hand from all parts of the County, and once again a special train carrying the bulk of the 2,000 spectators picked up from the usual railway stations along the way before heading off to St. Enoch's in Glasgow for their transfer to Ayr. In entering the ground, the 'Dale support swelled the capacity to around 10,000, and they most certainly made their presence felt as they gave the players a rousing reception on entering the field. During the week leading up to the match, the Armadale officials strengthened the team by making three new signings, with Scoullar, Gordon and Anderson replacing McCaig, Sullivan and Fleming.

Armadale started the match in determined fashion dominating the first fifteen minutes. Ayr eventually came into the match and they too had a dominant spell, but it was to be Armadale who opened the scoring, when the Ayr keeper was caught in "two minds" as he came out to clear the ball, allowing Gordon to stroke the ball home. Just before half time Ayr were unlucky as they hit the woodwork, but there was no further scoring as the half-time whistle sounded.

The second half started, and right away Armadale showed they had no intentions of sitting back on their lead, as the 'Dale forward line continued to create chance after chance, the best of them falling to Poole, who saw his effort hit the crossbar. Ayr had their moments, but as the game progressed, Armadale continued to play with great determination and deservedly held on till the final whistle, to record a remarkable 1-0 victory and make the *Glasgow News* (prophet) eat his words.

The scenes after the final whistle were unbelievable, as the West Lothian contingent in the crowd went mad with delight, cheering and shaking hands with one another as they rushed onto the field. Armadale players were all "chaired" and carried from the pitch to the pavilion. When news filtered back to the County, men and women took to the streets, not just in Armadale but also Bathgate, Broxburn, Bo'ness and Linlithgow. Even in Edinburgh newspaper placards advertised Armadale's victory. In the Broxburn Picturedome the result flashed up on the screen and was greeted with an enthusiastic and prolonged applause by the large audience. The management of Armadale Pavilion and of Bathgate Cinema House arranged to show part of the match, which in turn attracted large crowds for several days. Armadale had now reached the quarter finals - a remarkable achievement by any standards considering the opposition they were up against. Once again "lady luck" was on Armadale's side as they were given another home tie. Armadale at this stage were now the last remaining non-league side, so another crack against one of Scotland's elite was no doubt going to create and break a few more records.

With Celtic and Rangers being paired in one of the quarter finals, a strong Kilmarnock side was probably the next best draw for the 'Dale. Prior to the game rain fell heavily, but this didn't seem to dampen the spirits of the large crowd that was already beginning to form a full three hours before kickoff. The grandstand was filled mainly with Killie supporters who had brought up a large following with them, the majority travelling by relief trains. As well as the local support, once again football supporters from around the district descended on Volunteer Park, also in attendance was a large party of wounded soldiers from the Edinburgh War Hospital at

Bangour. With every available space in the ground taken up, the attendance must have been close on 10,000.

Armadale fielded the same eleven who disposed of Ayr, and suitably filled with gusto, took their chances against Kilmarnock who won the toss and took advantage of the incline. With the game played at a tremendous pace, there was very little between the sides, and it wasn't until the half hour mark before the deadlock was finally broken in controversial circumstances. Kilmarnock's J Smith chested the ball towards the goal, only for Robb to fist the ball clear on the goal line. The referee however adjudged that the ball had crossed the line, and barely two minutes later, Kilmarnock added a second through Culley. Once again Armadale looked hard done by as a few of the Killie forwards appeared to be in an offside position.

Less than five minutes after the restart, Gordon scrambled the ball home to give the 'Dale a lifeline. The home side enjoyed the majority of the second half, but were unable to penetrate the Killie defence. With a little luck, the home side could at the very least have forced a replay, but at the end of the day Kilmarnock held on to their slender lead and Armadale's cup dream was over. If there was to be any consolation for Armadale's cup run, it was the fact that Kilmarnock went on to lift the trophy. Full time: Armadale 1 Kilmarnock 2.

THE BIGGER PICTURE

Albion Rovers shocked Rangers in the semi finals with a 2-0 victory at Celtic Park, after 1-1 and 0-0 draws. Kilmarnock defeated Morton 3-2 in the other tie at Hampden. Kilmarnock then went on to collect the trophy for the first time with another 3-2 win, in front of an amazing crowd of 100,000. This was to be Albion Rovers only cup final appearance.

Season 1920-21 saw the four West Lothian sides enter the Qualifying Cup for what was to be the last time for a number of seasons. All four clubs were members of the Central League, but this was all to change at the end of the season as the Central League was to be scrapped and a new Scottish League Division Two was to be formed. This in turn meant that all the clubs would have automatic entry into the Scottish Cup.

74

Nevertheless, the Qualifying Cup got under way, in a final farewell to the competition it was rather refreshing to see the Edinburgh sides that had handed out several defeats to the County teams over the years eventually be on the receiving end for a change. Bo'ness hammered Leith Athletic 6-0, while Armadale defeated St. Bernards 3-0, with both games played at home. The final tie of the round saw Broxburn United win by the only goal of the game against Bathgate at the Sports Park. Bo'ness continued to find the net with another convincing 5-0 home win over Gala Fairydean. Armadale had a fine 3-1 win away to Berwick Rangers, while Broxburn United received a bye. All clubs made it by the third round, with Broxburn defeating Peebles Rovers 2-0, the other pair both receiving byes.

The fourth round saw a 2-1 victory for Armadale against Stenhousemuir, and yet another bye for Bo'ness. Broxburn went down 1-0 to Alloa Athletic away. Once again, Alloa did the damage recording a 2-0 home win over Armadale, leaving only Bo'ness to carry the flag for the County. After defeating Arbroath 2-1, they followed it up with victories over East Stirlingshire 2-0 then a 1-0 semi final win over Stevenson United.

A record crowd of just under 19,000 gathered at Central Park, Cowdenbeath for the final between Bo'ness and East Fife, and it was fully expected that Bo'ness would retain the trophy for the County. On a pitch that was frost bound and treacherous, Bo'ness made the mistake of trying to play close passing football, while the Methil men used the long ball tactic, which worked to their advantage. As it turned out, Bo'ness went down 3-1, but it took a last minute goal before East Fife sealed the victory.

The first round draw for the Scottish Cup saw a home tie for Bo'ness against Ayrshire side Galston. The weather was anything but favourable, as a strong south westerly wind would prove difficult to play good football. Tait scored the only goal of the game for Bo'ness midway through the second half, to send the majority of the 3,000 crowd home happy.

With Broxburn United receiving a bye into the next round, the remaining game of the round saw Armadale visit Paisley to take on First Division St. Mirren. There was considerable interest shown for this match after Armadale's surprise run in the last year's competition, and the attendance peaked at 8,000, with over 1,500 travelling from Armadale. With a strong wind on their backs, the home side opened the scoring after ten minutes. The first half was mainly all St. Mirren, but it was the visitors who found the net before half time, with a well taken goal from Wardrop. The second half kicked off, and as expected it was now Armadale's turn to take advantage of the windy conditions. Time after time the 'Dale dominated, but just when their prospects appeared bright, the unexpected happened and they found themselves trailing once more. 'Dale's keeper Short rushed out of goal to collect, but stumbled and fell on top of the ball and was pounced upon by two or three St. Mirren forwards. It seemed as if a foul should have been awarded, but as the ball broke free it was chipped into the empty net, with the keeper lying injured. This seemed to spur Armadale on, but too many chances went begging. With Wardrop, Dunsire and Kelly all missing open goals, it looked as if time was running out. Their determination however was rewarded with just under ten minutes remaining, when Dunsire made amends by levelling the match. By now Armadale went all out for that winning goal, and within four minutes Wardrop crashed the ball home from twenty yards to secure a marvellous 3-2 victory.

In a way, it was sad to see both Armadale and Bo'ness paired together for the second round of the competition, as it meant an early exit for one of the West Lothian clubs. On the other hand, it added a bit more spice to the tie, and a special train was run from Armadale picking up at Bathgate and Westfield. Cars and buses were also at hand to cope with the 1,500 or so Armadale supporters. In and around the Bo'ness area the game also caught the eye of football enthusiasts, with a large contingent travelling over from Grangemouth and Falkirk, thus swelling the gates in the region of around 6,000.

The game itself was hugely disappointing, with the home side having the bulk of play, but failing to find a way past a well drilled Armadale defence, but when it was breached, the Bo'ness forwards found keeper Short in fine form. Armadale supporters must have been bitterly disappointed with their side's contribution, but would have left somewhat happy that they held out for another chance at the Volunteer, as the game finished goalless.

Once again thousands of football supporters from all over the district made their way to Armadale. It was now Bo'ness' turn to travel and like the previous week a special train was laid on and with many others arriving by bus and car, in total around 1,500 arrived from the seaside town to swell the attendance to over 9,000. Armadale took advantage of the incline, and within the first few minutes you could see that they meant business as they homed in on the Bo'ness goal. Most of the 'Dale attacks were coming down the right wing with Weir and Speirs causing the Bo'ness defence continuous problems. With twenty five minutes on the clock, Armadale eventually opened the scoring with a fine goal from Williamson. Bo'ness responded immediately, a Clark drive grazing the post as Bo'ness continued to put pressure on the home defence, but there was no further scoring as the half time whistle sounded. Bo'ness started the second half brightly, but it was to be Armadale who gained control, and were unlucky not to increase their lead, as the ball hit the woodwork on a few occasions. However, with fifteen minutes remaining, Wardrop wrapped up the tie with a second goal after a fine run by Speirs.

The other second round tie attracted between 5,000 and 6,000 at the Sports Park in Broxburn, where Hamilton Academicals were visitors. With Accies leading 1-0 at half time, went on to increased their lead on the hour mark. Broxburn were far from out of the game and were awarded a penalty, and although Dunn missed the kick, he was quick enough to net the rebound and set up an exciting finish. United did come close to equalising on a few occasions, but it was not to be their day and the score remained 2-1 to the Lanarkshire club.

A home tie against First Division Albion Rovers, and indeed last season's finalists was enough to whet the appetite of the West Lothian football enthusiasts. The Armadale directors wisely arranged for the embankments around the ground to be increased, and despite this extra provision the ground once again easily reached its new capacity. Just before the game kicked off, around 12,000 spectators were in the ground and this was certainly helped on by a massive Coatbridge support. With just over fifteen minutes of the game played, Armadale were two goals up through Spiers and Sneddon. However, the homesters seemed to ease off a little and Rovers managed to pull level before half-time. Although there was no further scoring, there were many close calls at both ends, but Armadale would have felt more than a little disappointed at not entering the next round. Final score; Armadale 2. Albion Rovers 2.

The following Saturday (26th Feb) saw the replay at Cliftonhill, which attracted 22,000 spectators. Armadale did have the better of the chances but the game once again finished in stalemate 0-0. On the Wednesday (2nd March) both teams tried again, this time the neutral venue of Hampden Park and a crowd of 12,000 saw out another 0-0 draw, which included thirty minutes of extra time. The following day the tie was eventually decided as 9,000 witnessed a 2-0 win for Rovers.

THE BIGGER PICTURE

For the second time in as many seasons, Rangers and Albion Rovers clashed in the semi-finals. There was to be no shock like the previous year as Rangers ran out 4-1 winners. In the other semi-final it took three matches between Heart of Midlothian and Partick Thistle to decide the tie, and after two 0-0 draws, Thistle entered the final with a 2-0 win, all matches played at Ibrox.

With just thirty minutes before the kick-off, Partick Thistle were still unsure what their final team would be because of a horrendous injury list that lay in front of them. They had struggled along to the final stage after being involved in no fewer than six replays in their four previous ties, but despite all of their problems, Thistle went on to lift the Cup, winning 1-0 for what was to be the only time in their history.

As mentioned previously, the four West Lothian clubs were now members of the Scottish Football League (Second Division), and were exempt from entering the Qualifying Cup. When the draw was made, it was quite clear that the tie of the round involving County clubs was the clash at Easter Road between Hibernian and Armadale. A huge following of over 2,000 travelled from West Lothian as the gate hit the 15,000 mark. Although Armadale went down 3-0, they were by no means disgraced and at times in the match it was difficult to distinguish which was the lower league side. It was during the first forty five minutes that the Dale gave a more convincing display, the forwards in particular were exhibiting delightful touches, but lacking penetrative power in front of goal and failed to take advantage. The half-time whistle blew with both clubs failing to break the deadlock.

The second half however was a different story, as within four minutes of the restart the home side took the lead. This seemed to give Hibernian

78

more confidence and they took control of the game, but it was not until the seventy-fifth minute that they scored to put the tie beyond doubt. Armadale battled on bravely until the finish but couldn't find a way past Hibs keeper Harper for at the very least a consolation.

Broxburn United were also drawn away from home, as they travelled to Tayside to take on Dundee Hibernian, who had also recently been elected into the Second Division. Despite miserable weather, a crowd of 5,000 gathered at Tannadice Park to witness the match. The first half was evenly balanced, with both teams creating plenty of chances. It was not until the thirty-fifth minute that United's Cairns slammed home the first goal in a crowded penalty area. Barely a minute after the restart Allan scored a second goal for the visitors. The game was played in a similar fashion to the first half, where both sides continues to create chances, but at the end there was to be no further scoring with Broxburn thoroughly deserving their 2-0 victory.

Bo'ness, who were also drawn away from home, managed to persuade Stranraer to give up their ground rights, but sadly for Stranraer the attendance did not come up to expectations, with only some 1,500 spectators being present. In a rather one sided affair, Bo'ness ran out easy winners and first-half goals from Flannigan and Wardrop had Bo'ness on easy street. The second half, Stranraer seemed content to direct their energies in keeping the score down, however Flannigan kept the visitors defence busy and added a further three goals to bring his tally up to four with Wardrop scoring his second to round off a 6-0 win for the Blues.

The final tie of the first round saw the visit of Helensburgh to Mill Park. With Bathgate being clear favourites to win the tie, they were certainly in for a shock as the visitors took them all the way before going down 3-2. Bathgate took the lead when O'Raw converted a penalty and by half-time the game was tied at 1-1. Into the second half, and second penalty kick for Bathgate was easily put away by Black and in the sixty-fifth minute, McConnell seemed to put the game beyond doubt by adding a third. In great cup style Helensburgh kept fighting on and within a few minutes of Bathgate's goal, were awarded a penalty. Hamill who had scored earlier shot past the post, but five minutes later he made amends by scoring his and Helensburgh's second. Up until the end of play, the visitors couldn't find the goal they much deserved.

In the second round, and all three sides were drawn against First Division opposition, but the tie of the round was without doubt Bathgate verses high-flying Falkirk at Mill Park. Not only had Falkirk took points off the Old Firm in league business, they had also just acquired the signature of Syd Puddefoot from West Ham United for a substantial fee. The player had played for Falkirk during the war years and with all the hype and fine weather conditions, it was no surprise that a record crowd of 10,000 spectators crammed into Mill Park to witness the match.

Bathgate forward Robertson received a bad leg injury within fifteen minutes of the match and was forced to leave the field of play on a few occasions throughout the match. This in turn put the home side under considerable pressure, and as expected the game was mainly dominated by Falkirk. The match looked to be heading for a goal-less draw with less than twelve minutes remaining, but Robertson who had been limping badly for most of the match chased after the ball, which seemed a lost cause. However, he caught it on the bye-line and beat two opponents before drilling the ball from an acute angle towards the net. The ball seemed to have cannoned off Falkirk's Hunter and trundled into the net. The goal that was the result of sheer determination on Robertson's part was received with the wildest enthusiasm from the home support. With time ticking away, Falkirk pressed forward but failed to trouble Bathgate's Wilkinson. As soon as the final whistle sounded, a large section of the home spectators invaded the field to congratulate hero Robertson. Unable to make his way to the dressing room, the player had to be escorted by club directors and Policemen. Seldom has a player received such an ovation at the Mill Park ground, but in these circumstances the veteran was well worthy of the compliment.

Bo'ness travelled to Shawfield to take on Clyde, poor defending by the visitors saw them go in at the interval 3-0 down. A further two goals from the home side, and a Martin goal for Bo'ness completed the scoring, but in all fairness, Bo'ness gave a much better display than the scoreline suggests.

Considering the lean time Broxburn United were going through, mainly down to unemployment in the district, the club could scarcely have been given a better fixture in the second round at least from a financial point of view, than a meeting with Heart of Midlothian. The Broxburn directors gave up home advantage and this turned out to be a wise move as an attendance of over 20,000 packed into Tynecastle Park. Broxburn made one new addition to their squad by signing Hearts reserve forward Blair, and the following team took to the field; *McNaughton, Adams, Jamieson, Coyle, Allan, Cairns, Hendry, Davies, Blair, Williamson and Dunn.*

The game kicked off with Hearts sporting their blue jerseys due to a colour clash. Hearts started well and in their first attack, Millar was at hand to knock the ball into the net, after Forbes effort had rebounded off the bar. Hearts continued to create chances but found McNaughton in great form. It wasn't all Hearts however, as Broxburn came more into the game and it was no surprise when newcomer Blair deservedly equalised. Up until half time, the visitors had slightly more of the play and were well worth being on level terms. On resumption of the second half, it was now Broxburn's time to turn on the heat. On the hour mark Williamson had to leave the field owing to a bad injury. During that time however, ten men Broxburn took the lead through Davies. Encouraged by their success, Broxburn continued to have the upper hand, and this was also helped by the return of Williamson. With less than twenty minutes remaining however, Broxburn's Cairns was attempting to clear a cross when the ball bounced up and struck his hand. The referee at once awarded Hearts a penalty for what appeared to be completely accidental and the penalty was scored to level the game at 2-2. The remainder of the match was keenly contested with both sides having chances to win, but there was to be no further scoring.

The replay was once again played at Tynecastle Park and for a midweek match; the attendance was surprisingly large, with close on 20,000 spectators in the ground. Broxburn certainly didn't lack support, with well wishers from all over the County, Bo'ness in particular being well represented. Broxburn were unchanged after keeper McNaughton, who was unwell just before kick-off, decided to take to the field. Hearts on the other hand made a couple of changes. Broxburn started the match in great style, dominating the first twenty-five minutes, and it was all United at this stage as they totally outplayed their first division opponents. After striking the woodwork on a couple of occasions, Broxburn deservedly took the lead in the twenty-eighth minute, when a delightful cross from Henry found Williamson who caught the ball on the drop and gave keeper Kane no chance, as the ball crashed in off the post. Broxburn continued to dominate and if it was not for the rough antics from the home side, the visitors could easily have tied up a third round visit of Rangers. As it often happens however, with only a couple of minutes of the first half remaining, Hearts equalised, with McNaughton beaten from close range. Within four minutes of the second half , Broxburn regained the lead as Williamson ran on to knock in a rebound. The lead lasted only a few minutes however, as Hearts equalled the scores, but the Broxburn players hotly disputed the goal, claiming that scorer Miller was in an off-side position. Play raged on from end to end for the remainder of the match, and Hearts continued their heavy handed antics, as Broxburn were forced to play the closing stages with ten men, as goal scorer Williamson was carried off the pitch. There was to be no more scoring as the game again finished in a 2-2 draw.

For the third match Broxburn were again unchanged for their visit to Tynecastle. A heavy snowfall during the night, and on the morning of the match, resulted in a smaller attendance from the previous games, but nonetheless a gate of around 15,000 was quite remarkable, with the County folk out in force to lend their support. Once again it was Broxburn who did all the early running, and it was no surprise when they took the lead within six minutes through Dunn, after clever footwork from Blair and Hendry. Unfortunately for Broxburn their lead was short lived, as Hearts equalised within a minute. Broxburn won three corners in quick succession, but all proved fruitless. Following the third corner, Meikle of Hearts raced away and drew out the entire Broxburn defence, before squaring to Forbes, who in turn had the easy job of knocking the ball into an empty net. Broxburn pressed hard for the equaliser, but the half time whistle sounded with Hearts leading 2-1.

After the break Broxburn continued where they had left off, most of the attacks coming from down the right side where Hendry was in outstanding form, creating many chances but failing to find the net. With only fifteen minutes remaining, disaster struck when Hearts broke downfield. As the ball crossed over, Hearts forward Forbes, who looked well offside, stroked the ball past the helpless McNaughton. At that stage Broxburn looked the more likely to score rather than lose more ground. With only a couple of minutes remaining, Broxburn were awarded a penalty after Williamson was sandwiched in the box, but Coyle's spot kick was too direct, and the keeper parried the ball round the post. In the final minute, Broxburn's luck deserted them once again, when a Hearts defender struck his own upright as he attempted to clear. At the end of the day the 3-1 score line flattered Hearts, where a third replay would have seemed a fairer result. Probably the most important aspect of the three matches was the financial side, which was most definitely a godsend to the cash stricken Broxburn side.

It was now all down to Bathgate as they journeyed to Firhill to take on Scottish Cup holders Partick Thistle. A crowd of 18,000 gathered for this match with around a 1,000 Bathgate supporters in attendance. Bathgate won the toss and took advantage of the wind and opened brightly, but with little more than five minutes on the clock, Bathgate received a set back as centre forward J Black was forced to leave the field due to injury. This in turn proved a huge disadvantage to Bathgate, as they still pressed forward creating chances but clearly missing Black's presence up front. Around the half hour mark Black returned but was clearly struggling as he limped around the pitch. Ten minutes before the interval Thistle took the lead, Bathgate's keeper Wilkinson injured his wrist while attempting to collect a cross and the ball was bundled into the net.

Surprisingly Bathgate started strong in the second half, but failed to find an equaliser. With twenty-five minutes remaining Thistle doubled their lead, and with only a few minutes remaining scored a third and final goal. In the end, the injury to Black was the turning point in the game, as there were never three goals between the sides.

THE BIGGER PICTURE

For a third year in succession a team was to win the Scottish Cup for the first time. A 3-1 victory for Morton against Aberdeen at Dens Park sent them on their way for a Hampden showdown with Rangers, following their 2-0 win over Partick Thistle. Like last year the game was decided by a single goal, Rangers keeper Robb handling outside the area, with Morton scoring from the resulting free kick.

Just like the previous year, the first round tie for 1922/23 season, Bo'ness hit their opponents for six. The unlucky team this time round was Highland League side Clachnacuddin. Weather was raw and cold with the playing surface in poor condition, as around 2,000 supporters watched on. Bo'ness taking no risks fielded their strongest team possible, and as the score line suggests was very much a one sided match. Four goals from Mackie and one apiece for Anderson and new signing Caldwell sent the "Blues" comfortably into the next round.

The only other West Lothian side to join Bo'ness into the next round was Bathgate, who needed a reply to dispose of East Stirlingshire. The first match played at Falkirk, as expected the weather conditions was similar to that at Bo'ness. Bathgate brought with them a large support of over 1,000 as the attendance reached the 4,000 mark, and they enjoyed lengthy spells of this match, more or less dominating the first half along with twenty minutes of the second, totally in control. Bathgate were only one goal to the good that coming from a penalty in the fifth minute after McAllister was brought down in the box, Pearson scoring the spot kick. With twenty minutes remaining, a second penalty was awarded this time to the home side, who made no mistake and squared the game at 1-1. This appeared to inspire the Falkirk side, as they fought hard for the winning goal, but the Bathgate defence stood firm to earn a replay.

The replay the following Wednesday afternoon attracted a similar crowd of around 4,000 to Mill Park. With great interest shown locally for this match, several of the Bathgate firms agreed after being approached by their workers, to grant time off to watch the match, with the time to be made up at the end of the week. In a keenly contested match, Bathgate's Drummond hit the back of the net three times, his second a spectacular overhead kick. The match finished 3-2 with East Stirlingshire's second goal coming moments before the final whistle.

Armadale travelled to Johnstone to take on their fellow Second Division opponents, a few weeks previous Armadale hammered Johnstone 7-2 in a league match at the Volunteer, so at the very least they were fully expected of at least a replay. As it turned out, Armadale for all their dominance in the match failed to score, with the game looking a certainty to finish goal less, Johnstone broke away twice in the last ten minutes to win the tie and book their place in the second round.

The final match of the first round saw Broxburn United travel to Rugby Park to take on First Division side Kilmarnock. Broxburn had keeper McKinlay to thank for keeping the score down to single figures as Kilmarnock strolled to a relaxing 5-0 victory, "Killies" Jackson hitting the target on four occasions.

The second round certainly brought some excitement to the County, when Bo'ness were rewarded with a home tie against Heart of Midlothian, while Bathgate visited Hampden Park to take on Queens Park, which was witnessed by the Duke of York.

First up was the match at Newtown Park, when the week leading up to the tie Hearts offered Bo'ness a substantial sum to waiver ground advantage. However the Bo'ness directors knocked back the offer. Immediately following that decision, the Bo'ness Board made an announcement that the ground admission was to be raised to two shillings, but this not only met with opposition from Hearts, but raised a storm of protests from the home supporters. In the end the Board backed down and reverted back to the customary charges.

Leading up to the game, embankments to the east and west of the ground were greatly heightened, while additional admission gates were built at the north-east corner of the ground, everything was in place for the anticipated bumper crowd. On the day, Hearts brought out a large contingent of around 4,000, many of whom arrived by one of three special trains, with supporters flocking in from all over the County, and the final attendance peaked in the region of 8,000 - 9,000.

The Bo'ness team that day were as follows;

Stevenson, Brown, Harris, Rayne, Anderson, Moffat, Clark, Kelly, Mackie, Dawson and Stewart.

Hearts won the toss and took advantage of a stiff westerly breeze. As imagined Hearts were the more dominate force, with twenty minutes on the clock they opened the scoring with a twenty yard drive from White. Up until half-time the match turned rather volatile, with Hearts being the main instigators. Play raged on, and tackle after tackle got worse, until it seemed as if the game was going to boil over, so much so that only nine of the Bo'ness team survived to the interval - Hearts only slightly better off with ten. However, all credit to the Blues as they stuck to their task and kept the score line down to just a single goal.

Both teams resumed at full strength, numerically at least, as a few players came out sporting bandages and plasters over their various injuries.

85

Bo'ness, now with the wind to their advantage opened strongly and continued to pin their opponents to their own half, and it was to be no surprise when just under ten minutes from the restart, Bo'ness' Kelly evaded a few hefty challenges to stroke the ball past Hearts keeper Gilfillan, to give the home team a deserved equaliser. The cheering after this goal was quite deafening, and lasted for a good few minutes. Bo'ness continued to dominate and it was all down to the woodwork and a string of good saves that kept the Edinburgh side in the match. With fifteen minutes remaining the home support went wild as Moffat hammered home a second goal to give Bo'ness the lead. However, a shock awaited them, as barely two minutes later Hearts equalised after a mix up between Brown and Anderson allowed Hearts centre forward White to level the scores. This prompted Bo'ness to double their efforts and their superiority became more pronounced as ever. It was to be no surprise therefore when Rayne restored their lead a few minutes later. As the final minutes ticked away, Bo'ness were in total command, with Brown being unlucky seeing his long range effort crash off the crossbar. Final score Bo'ness 3 Heart of Midlothian 2.

Seldom, if ever, had an Association football game aroused so much widespread interest as did the Queens Park v Bathgate second round tie at Hampden Park. In itself the tie was no more attractive than any other in the round, but the fact that royalty in the form of the Duke of York was to be present, placed the event right in the forefront, and converted the match into quite a social occasion.

In Bathgate and surrounding districts, the tie was generally regarded as being the biggest that the Bathgate club had ever participated in, so much so that around 2,500 - 3,000 people travelled through to Hampden from West Lothian, with Provost Walker and members of the Bathgate Town Council also in attendance. The weather leading up to the match was unfortunately dull, with constant drizzle, but this did not dampen the enthusiasm of those who attended, when the final attendance figure rose to around 60,000.

The Bathgate team which took to the field on this special occasion was as follows;

Stewart, Fergus, Gilmour, Harley, Robertson, Pearson, Cornelius, McAllister, Drummond, McConnell and Black.

The game itself was a bit of a letdown, probably due to nerves, as both clubs took time to settle, with Bathgate looking the more likely, using the wind to their advantage. Finally after thirty minutes on the clock, McAllister broke the deadlock with a shot from close range. The same player moments later should have put the West Lothian men further in front, after beating three men, he only had the goalkeeper to beat, but his shot was too direct and the keeper was able to divert the ball over the bar. Into the second half and Bathgate seemed to be sitting comfortable on their slender lead. Twenty minutes into the second half Bathgate were unfortunate not to be given a penalty kick. After a most glaring infringement, Black was blatantly pushed off the ball, but being in such a good position to the referee, played advantage and the chance went a begging. That decision came back to haunt Bathgate as within a few minutes Queens Park were on level terms. From there on in, both teams had chances to win the tie, McAllister in particular missing an open goal, but there was to be no more scoring, as the match ended Queens Park 1 Bathgate 1.

A record crowd was expected for the visit of Queens Park to Mill Park. Once again local works suspended operations to allow employees to witness the match, but unfortunately the weather broke down in the afternoon and rain fell heavily for the duration of the match, in total only 6,000 supporters braved the elements. In what turned out to be a poor match, Queens Park adapted better to the heavy playing surface, with Bathgate failing to reproduce anything like their form on the Saturday. After a goalless first half, Queens found the net twice in the second to record a 2-0 victory.

Bo'ness were once again drawn against "non-league" opposition, this time round saw Dumfriesshire side Nithsdale Wanderers visit Newtown Park. Wanderers had previously knocked out Second Division sides Arbroath and Dundee Hibernian, so it was fair to say Bo'ness were not going to be treating their Sanquhar guests cheaply. A Caldwell goal after only six minutes gave Bo'ness the lead, but it was not until the sixty-fifth minute before Bo'ness scored their second goal, Clark scoring from the penalty spot after Caldwell had been fouled in the box. Bo'ness certainly not playing to their best, had some anxious moments as the plucky Southerners fought all the way to the final whistle. There was no further scoring, and the blues entered the last eight of the competition for the first time.

When the fourth round draw was made, Bo'ness' name came out the hat second, this meant that the club would have to travel for the first time, with a trip to Fir Park, to take on First Division side Motherwell. On a fine sunny day, an attendance of well over 15,000, around 2,000 of whom had travelled from West Lothian. The home side dominated early proceedings and after only seven minutes Bo'ness found themselves 1-0 down. Motherwell continued to press on the Bo'ness defence and it was no surprise when they added a second, with only eighteen minutes into the game. This second goal was a wake-up call for Bo'ness, and after a good spell of pressure managed to pull a goal back nearing the half-hour mark, when a powerful shot from Kelly was dropped by the Motherwell keeper. Mackie was quick to pounce, and placed the ball into the corner of the net. This seemed to liven the game up with both sides creating many chances, with just under four minutes to half-time, Motherwell added a third after good work from the left. Half-time - Motherwell 3 Bo'ness 1.

Bo'ness started the second half in a lively fashion creating many chances but failing to find the net. A strong penalty appeal was also turned down as Stewart, who was clean through, was brought down right on the eighteen yard line. A free kick was awarded at the edge of the box but proved fruitless. With only fifteen minutes remaining, Motherwell secured their fourth goal. Bo'ness were now in a hopeless position and their misfortunes were increased when Brown was ordered off following a bust up with Motherwell's Reid. A penalty goal in the closing minutes by Clark gave the final score a more respectable look. At the end of the day Bo'ness were due a lot of credit in the manner that they never gave up until the final whistle. Full time - Motherwell 4 Bo'ness 2

THE BIGGER PICTURE

Motherwell went down 2-0 at Ibrox to Celtic, while the other semi-final tie played at Tynecastle saw Hibernian defeat Third Lanark 1-0. Celtic ran out 1-0 winners in the final.

With three out of the four clubs travelling away from home, support for these clubs was going to be at a minimum due to a National Rail strike.

Broxburn supporters arranged a special train, which would have saw around 500-600 fans make the trip to Kirkcaldy to take on Raith Rovers. The "gate" was pretty reasonable all the same with 9,000 present. In hindsight, it was probably just as well the Broxburn support missed out on this one, as the whole match turned out to be a dour, drab affair. Rovers seemed to take Broxburn cheaply, and indeed the visitors seemed to be infected with the same lack of interest. By the end of the day Rovers ran out 3-0 winners in a very disappointing encounter.

Armadale made the long journey south to take on amateur side Coldstream. With no trains available, Armadale set off by bus along with around forty supporters, leaving the town at 7.30am for the lengthy trip. A record crowd of 600 gathered into the tiny Home Park, where another poor game was witnessed. Although Armadale never looked like losing this tie, the more the match went on, the more likely a replay would be needed to separate the sides. However, with little more than ten minutes remaining, a cross from Speirs led to a scrimmage in the goalmouth, in which Meikle managed to bundle both the ball and the goalkeeper into the net for the only goal of the game.

The final tie of the round saw County rivals Bathgate and Bo'ness clash at Mill Park. The tie brought a great deal of excitement to the area in the build up to the match. With two special trains booked to take the majority of the "Blues" support, other ways and means had to be found to take the large support, and by 10.30am crowds had began to assemble at the foot of the wynd as motor vehicles of all descriptions lined up to cater for the growing numbers, with many of the vehicles making several trips, others making their way by foot and bicycle.

The match kicked off in front of 7,000 spectators and for a game which expected so much, delivered very little. The game ended 1-1 with both goals coming in the first half with Bathgate taking the lead twelve minutes after the start, a long hard drive from Robertson caught the Bo'ness defence by surprise. With Drummond arriving on the scene, he diverted the ball past keeper Hilligan and into the net via the inside of the post. The equaliser came fifteen minutes later when Wardrop latched onto a cross from the right and placed the ball well out of the reach of goalkeeper Stewart.

Into the second half and it was Bathgate who had the bulk of the match, but unable to score that elusive second goal - the closest they came was a Drummond header that came off the crossbar. Bo'ness were happy enough to sit back and clear their lines, adapting time-wasting tactics as defenders frequently kicked the ball out of the ground, much to the disgust of the home support. At the end of the day Bathgate would have been the more disappointed throwing away home advantage, whilst Bo'ness on the other hand with their "no risk" attitude probably just deserved a share of the spoils. The replay on the Wednesday afternoon saw another bumper crowd, as schools and public works closed down early. In an exciting end to end game, only a Brown penalty for Bo'ness separated the sides, more penalties should have been awarded to the home side, the game would have been over as a contest by the first half.

The second round saw both Armadale and Bo'ness visit Glasgow. For the second year in succession a West Lothian club were drawn in the second round against Queens Park at Hampden, with Armadale being the visitors to the famous ground. Despite the fact the 'Dale didn't have members of the Royal Family in attendance and that rain fell before and during the match, the gate was quite satisfactory, with attendance being estimated at around 15,000. Leading up to the tie Armadale, in a bid to strengthen the team for the occasion signed Grainger from Celtic, along with Smellie late of Heart of Midlothian and St. Mirren. It was not a great game so far as football was concerned; play was too keen to allow much of the finer points of the game to shine through. The players did show a lot of vigour and enthusiasm, which made the contest an interesting one. Queens deservedly took the lead after eighteen minutes, a powerful shot that keeper Short managed to get his fingertips to, but was unable to keep the ball out of the net. After the goal there seemed a lot more urgency in Armadale's play, with new signing Grainger skimming the crossbar on a couple of occasions. Eventually Armadale equalised through Ashton before the interval, his neat shot ending up in the corner of the net. Into the second half and it took Queens little under nine minutes to restore the lead. After this, play was very much uneventful, with midfield dominating the game, leaving both keepers with very little to do. With just under ten minutes remaining, the home side secured victory with a third and final goal. While there was no denying the fact the honours ultimately went to the better side, Armadale put up a very creditable show, and at one stage in the match looked like a replay was inevitable.

The other match saw Bo'ness visit Firhill to take on Partick Thistle, with the match ending 3-0 to the home side. Partick found their West Lothian opponents a difficult proposition and for over an hour the game hung in the balance. As a matter of fact, if Bo'ness had stuck away a gilt-edged opportunity just before Thistle opened the scoring, the result may have been very different. That goal came in sixty-five minutes followed by a second nine minutes later, and the final goal scored in the last minute of the game, gave the home side a very flattering victory.

Bo'ness FC 1923 group photo © Falkirk Archives

THE BIGGER PICTURE

After two 0-0 draws Hibernian finally overcame Aberdeen to book the second successive final, winning 1-0, with all matches played at Dens Park. Airdrieonians defeated Falkirk in the other tie, with a 2-1 win at Celtic Park. A Willie Russell double gave Airdrieonians their first and only Scottish Cup win at Ibrox Park.

Season 1924-25 saw three out of the four West Lothian sides take on lower or non-league teams in the first round of the Scottish Cup. It was Bathgate who were to have the toughest tie at home, Partick Thistle were to prove too strong a side for the Mill Park outfit. A visit from a First Division club is always welcomed in provincial circles. In this instance, the belief was pretty widespread that Bathgate would be capable of giving Thistle a close run, with the most common forecast amongst the home following being a draw. How much the home side's supporters were to be disappointed though, as Bathgate put on one of their worst displays for many a year, and as a consequence the visitors had a comparatively easy passage into the next round. Three nil ahead at half-time, the game was wrapped up after just under the hour mark when the fourth and final goal was scored.

With the remaining County teams all having home ties against lower opposition, all made it through to the second round. Armadale saw off non-leaguers Civil Service Strollers 3-1 without having to get into "second gear", Strollers scoring their consolation goal minutes from the end from the penalty spot. Broxburn were drawn against eventual Third Division champions Nithsdale Wanderers, a replay always seemed on the cards as the teams were locked at 2-2, but late in the game Broxburn's Hair made it 3-2. Just on the final whistle Coyle had a chance to put the match beyond doubt, but struck his spot kick well over the bar. The final tie for the round saw Bo'ness struggle to overcome Third Division Helensburgh. With home advantage it seemed unlikely that Bo'ness would entail any problems, but a stuffy Helensburgh side matched their hosts all the way in the first half, and it was little surprise when they took the lead moments before the interval. The second half as imagined was dominated by the home side that quickly equalised through Cottingham. With the prospect of a midweek trip to Helensburgh, the "Blues" pressed hard to get an important second, but the visitors stood firm, and honours were even. The replay at Helensburgh failed to separate the sides and the game finished goal-less. The following Tuesday 4000 fans watched on at Partick Thistle's Firhill Park, where Bo'ness eventually secured a second round visit to Kirkcaldy, a Kelly header within four minutes settling the nerves, but it took until the sixty-fifth minute before the tie was safe, when a Stewart lob found its way into the net. Helensburgh continued to fight on, but poor finishing ended their hopes of any comeback as the game finished 2-0 in Bo'ness' favour.

The tie of the second round was without doubt the match at Volunteer Park between Armadale and Aberdeen. Less than expected watched the match with supporters from the other County clubs staying loyal to their teams. Nevertheless around 8,000 turned up to watch the match, with Aberdeen directors putting on a special train, only 65 supporters bothered to turn up, which meant a financial loss to the visiting club as it did not meet a 200 guarantee as was expected.

In a keenly fought cup tie, Armadale had the ball in the net early on, but was rightly disallowed for an infringement. The home support however had something to cheer about as Chisholm opened the scoring, a shot from Leitch was caught by a freak gust of wind and as the ball curled away from goal, it landed perfectly at the foot of Chisholm who in turn blasted the ball into the back of the net. Both teams upped the pace and the 'Dale were looking for that killer second, while the 'Dons fought for an equaliser. It was to be the latter that had success as Pirie headed home from two yards, which looked suspiciously offside. The second half was also keenly played with Armadale having the slightly better of the match, but in the end a trip to Aberdeen always seemed the outcome.

The replay on the Wednesday was watched by 17,000 spectators at Pittodrie, where around 300 'Dale supporters made the long journey. Aberdeen totally dominated the match, but only two first half strikes from Pirie was all Aberdeen had for their efforts. All credit was due to 'Dale keeper Davis who brought out some outstanding saves and keeping the score line respectable.

Bo'ness also met First Division opposition as they took on Raith Rovers at Starks Park. A well drilled Bo'ness defence held up well to record a 0-0 draw and the 'Blues were seldom on the attack, seemingly quite happy to soak up the homesters pressure and take their chances at the Newtown. The replay was more closely contested, as the game was played in a more cup-tie fashion. Both clubs created chances, but it was to be Rovers who took a 1-0 interval lead. On the hour mark, Bo'ness deservedly equalised through Kelly, but it was to be Raith who regained their lead with fifteen minutes remaining. The game was wrapped up in the closing minutes with a third and final goal.

The final match of the round saw Broxburn United travel to Larkhall to take on Third Division Royal Albert. Broxburn opened strongly, giving the home defence problems with their aggressive tactics, so it was to be no surprise when Coyle gave the visitors the lead after only ten minutes. The Larkhall side did manage to equalise via the penalty spot, but Broxburn's Wardrop regained the lead with a well taken goal before half time. The second half and the game continued to be keenly and stubbornly contested with hard knocks being frequent on both sides. A third goal from Walker secured victory for Broxburn and with a two goal cushion, United never relaxed their grip of the game, with an effort from Dixon striking the post near the end, but Broxburn ran out worthy winners with a little to spare.

A home draw in the third round against first leaguers Falkirk was the prize for Broxburn, as 9,000 supporters crammed into the Sports Park. In a very entertaining match, the home side just edged home with a 2-1 victory. With little more than eight minutes on the clock, Broxburn's Hair glanced home a header in off the post, after fine work from Walker down the left side. Broxburn continued to have the better of the first half, but although having a few good chances, failed to increase their lead. Into the second half and it was now Falkirk's turn to add some pressure, as home defence had a few lucky escapes in the opening second period, when eventually on the hour mark the game was level with Todd scoring from close range in off the post. With both teams going all out for victory, luck fell to Broxburn as centre forward Graham headed home the winner. Falkirk's keeper got his fingers to the ball but failed to grip it properly and it appeared to slip out of his grasp and fall into the empty net. It was a shot that keeper Ferguson should have saved. The home support knew no bounds and men and women kissed each other with joy. The game still had several minutes to go as Falkirk pressed hard for the equaliser, but good defending from the home side, Reid in particular saving the day on a few occasions, held out to record a memorable victory.

Broxburn United were now in the last eight, and also the last team from the lower leagues left in the competition. Avoiding the Old Firm, Broxburn were drawn against Dundee at Dens Park and a chance of progressing to the semi-final stages was certainly on the cards. It was unfortunate that Broxburn had to take to the field with two of their players not altogether fit. Front man Coyle was recovering from influenza, and Walker still suffering from a knock against Falkirk. Both players showed no lack of effort, but it was evident at times, as they did not show their usual characteristics in their play.

On the day of the match a special train picked up supporters starting at Bathgate with the largest contingent, as expected from Uphall and Broxburn, but Livingston, Ratho and Dalmeny each sent a fair amount of

94

enthusiasts to lend their support. Unfortunately there was some delay at Dalmeny station and the fully packed train with over 1100 arrived at Dundee Station just before three o'clock. Word soon got through to the ground and asking for a delay to the kick-off, but the Dens Park officials showed little consideration and went ahead as they had planned. This in turn meant that Broxburn's large following were a full fifteen minutes late in entering the ground. Nothing was missed however, in a very disappointing match, and Broxburn certainly failed to produce anything like their best form.

Although their defence stood firm, a fully fit forward line would most certainly have been more than enough to have ousted a poor Dundee side out of the Cup. United held out until the seventy-fifth minute. At a time when a replay at the Sports Park seemed imminent, as a corner was swung over, keeper McKinlay was fouled, but unfortunately for United the referee failed to see any infringement, as the home side took advantage by slamming the ball into the net. To finish on a brighter note, Broxburn took home a share of the £616 gate money from the 15,500 in attendance.

THE BIGGER PICTURE

Celtic thrashed rivals Rangers 5-0 at Hampden, while Dundee and Hamilton saw out a 1-1 draw at Tynecastle, Dundee eventually won the replay 2-0 at Easter Road. Celtic went on to record their eleventh trophy win, beating Dundee 2-1 at Hampden.

The top draw for the first round of the 1925-26 Scottish Cup for County clubs was no doubt Broxburn United's visit into Edinburgh to play Hibernian. Although the Easter Road men were struggling away in the lower reaches of the First Division, a crowd of over 14,000 gathered, where a share of the £475 gate money was most welcome for the financially stricken Broxburn side. Over 1,000 supporters, many of whom had walked the eleven or so miles, greeted the visitors as they took to the field, the team sporting their new strip, maroon jerseys with a narrow green neckband and white shorts (kindly donated by the Broxburn Supporters Club).

Broxburn were certainly up for the fight and opened aggressively, displaying real cup tie enthusiasm. There was no fancy stuff as their "up and at 'em" tactics paid off. After as little as three minutes on the clock, a Raeburn free kick dinged the net in off the post, after being deflected along the way, giving the Hibs keeper no chance. This was certainly a wake-up call for the home side. Although they dominated for much of the first half, Broxburn defence stayed firm and deservedly lead at the interval. With the second half under way, it was evident that the home side were all out to quickly level the scores as they put pressure on the visiting goal. It paid off when within eight minutes a Miller header found the net. This reverse was a spur-on rather than a dampener for Broxburn, as they proceeded to make a sustained attack on the Hibernian goal. The closest they came was a Taylor drive, which rebounded back into play after coming off the bar. It was indeed a life for the Hibs, but they managed to survive the onslaughts of their Second Division opponents. Hibs could easily have stolen the tie, as they squandered a brilliant chance in the dying minutes. In the end it was all credit to Broxburn who were well worthy of a second chance.

In view of a generous offer from the Hibernian board, United decided to replay the tie once again at Easter road. The official Broxburn Supporters Club were also looked after, with free entry into the ground. Although Broxburn never struck quite as good a game as they did on the Saturday, they made Hibs fight all the way for their victory. After an evenly matched first half, Hibernian opened the scoring within four minutes of the restart which turned out to be the only goal of the game. Both teams squandered great opportunities, but it was to be Broxburn who almost snatched an equaliser right at the death, where a half-hour extra-time could not have been grudged to them.

The other three ties involving the County clubs were all Second Division affairs, two of which produced 5-4 score lines.

Bathgate's home tie against East Stirlingshire was one such game that produced nine goals, and plenty of goalmouth incidents keeping the 3,000 crowd well entertained. Goals from Scoular (2) and McKinlay gave Bathgate a 3-1 lead after just over fifty minutes on the clock. Much to the surprise of the home support, instead of the Shires heads going down, it was quite the opposite as they suddenly developed a "never say die" spirit. Two goals, within a ten minute spell of Bathgate securing their fifth, certainly brought some life back into the game. However   Bathgate regrouped, and although the final score suggests a close match, Shire fourth goal came with the last kick of the ball.

The other game producing nine goals took place at Barrhead, where Arthurlie were hosts to Armadale. The game was played in terrible conditions, with the pitch being described as a mud bath. Trailing 4-2 at half time, Armadale came out fighting in the second half and deservedly levelled the game at 4-4. Chances went a begging as Armadale pushed forward for the winner, but it was to be Arthurlie who were to score the decisive fifth goal in a game where a draw would have been the fairer outcome.

Finally East Fife visited Newtown Park, but heavy rain prior to the kick-off left the pitch in a soft and slippery state. East Fife, with a westerly breeze behind them, were happy to shoot on sight of goal, but with a rather far from convincing display, were only one goal up at the interval, the goal coming after thirty-six minutes. Bo'ness resumed in strong fashion after the break, taking a leaf out of East Fife's book striking the ball towards goal whenever possible. Their reward came after eighteen minutes, when fine play by Millar rounded the Fifers defence before squaring to Cottingham, who made no mistake. Excitement now raged round the ropes as both clubs went all out for the winner.

With fifteen minutes remaining, and the light none too good and the pitch cut up badly, it seemed a draw would be the likely result. Tactics from the Fifers at this stage suggested that nothing would have suited them better, but the home side had other ideas, and in the eightieth minute, Martin, who had been waiting on his chance, cleverly scored the winning goal. The game finished in a downpour with thick mist surrounding the ground. East Fife fought desperately for that equaliser but it never came as Bo'ness ran out 2-1 winners.

With only two West Lothian clubs still in the competition it was rather unlucky that both clubs were drawn against each other. With Bo'ness having home advantage and playing the better football at that time, they were clear favourites to progress into the third round. Early in the game it was Bo'ness who were doing most of the pressing, but bad finishing from Martin and the scoreline remained blank. In the twenty-seventh minute Martin made amends by nipping in and finishing off after a well placed corner was headed on by Hair. Just on half-time Martin was up to his old tricks; with an open goal at his mercy, the forward somehow managed to put the ball past the post. At this stage it would have certainly put the match out of Bathgate's reach. The second half got under way with the game swinging from end to end, and the latter stages of the game were all Bathgate. However their efforts seemed doomed to disappointment, into the final seconds of the match and many supporters having left the ground, they missed out on Pearson scoring a dramatic equaliser. So late was the goal scored that there was no time to centre the ball. Over the ninety Bo'ness had the bulk of play, but missed chances cost them dearly. The replay attracted a similar attendance to that of the first match, 3.500 with around 100 making the trip over from Bo'ness.

Bathgate enjoyed most of the first half hour, but failed to make any impact – closest they came was in the twenty-ninth minute when McKinlay struck the post. Within a minute Bo'ness snatched the lead through Martin after a defensive mix up. Bathgate continued to put pressure on the visitor's goal and within five minutes were on level terms through Scoular. Just on half-time Bo'ness had a penalty claim turned away when Bathgate's Gay handled in the box, but the referee waved away the visitors appeals. Five minutes after the restart a Pearson free kick sailed into the top right corner of the net, giving Bo'ness keeper Reid no chance. Both teams continued to create chances but as the game wore on, it was to be Bathgate who were to wrap up the game, with a third goal, and Pearson once again finding the net to complete the scoring.

Airdrieonians supplied the opposition for the third round tie at Mill Park. The counter attractions at Edinburgh (Hearts v Celtic) and at Falkirk (Falkirk v Rangers) had an adverse effect on the attendance. However a couple of special trains brought in large contingents from Airdrie, in addition to those who have travelled by road, which helped raise the attendance to over 7,000. Bathgate opened brightly, with Airdrie Keeper Ewart being well tested in the opening fifteen minutes, but a minute later he had to acknowledge defeat, as Weir slammed home the opener after good work down the right flank. Bathgate continued to find openings in the visitors defence, but the Diamonds continued to monopolise the play, without showing any real threat. Somerville in particular causing the Bathgate defence most problems, so it was no surprise when the left winger hit a low drive eight minutes from the interval. Within a minute, slack defending from the home side allowed Somerville to grab his second, which seemed tough luck on Bathgate, who had looked like holding out until half time.

Airdrie were much more in the game after the resumption, and had now taken a firm grip of the match. Bathgate were seldom seen on the attack as Airdrie carved open the home defence. On the hour mark Somerville got his hat-trick scoring from an acute angle. A few minutes later the game was all but over, as that man Somerville notched his and Airdrie's fourth. Play had now deteriorated with Airdrie happy to sit back on their three goal cushion, and with less than five minutes remaining, Anderson got a fifth for the visitors. This was not the last however, with Scoular scoring a consultation goal for Bathgate just on the final whistle. Result; Bathgate 2 Airdrieonians 5.

THE BIGGER PICTURE

Celtic defeated Aberdeen 2-1 at Tynecastle, while St. Mirren marched into the final defeating Rangers 1-0. St. Mirren went on to lift the trophy for the first time defeating Celtic 2-0.

For the first time since 1920 a West Lothian side participated in the Scottish Qualifying Cup. It was all down to Broxburn United losing their league status finishing bottom of the Second Division. With the Third Division folding, Broxburn had no choice other than to join the Scottish Alliance. The writing was on the wall as the club struggled with falling attendances, due to the economic depression. The town of Broxburn was badly affected with mines and oil works closing, causing mass redundancies.

Broxburn did reasonably well reaching the last eight of the competition, eventually going down 3-1 to Inverness Caledonian away – this was enough to book their place in the Scottish Cup proper.

A home tie against Armadale was the outcome, with the match watched by over 2,500 spectators – a record crowd for Broxburn that season. It took the visitors only six minutes to find the net, when neat work from Martin found Young, who cleverly knocked the ball home. Within a few minutes Broxburn were unlucky not to equalise, when a McBurnie effort struck the base of the post. Armadale had the bulk of the first half, but their forcible play saw them penalised on several occasions as they struggled to find that important second goal. With the interval fast approaching, a long range effort from Reid found the back of the net, to give Broxburn an equaliser. Eight minutes into the second half and Broxburn surprised the 'Dale by taking the lead. This came from a solo run from Simpson, that ended with him lashing out from a distance, the ball high in the air was left by keeper Davis, who was taken by surprise as the ball dipped and ended up in the back of the net. From there on, Broxburn played a wise defensive game, taking no risks as Armadale fought hard for the equaliser, but is was non league Broxburn's day as they held out to record a fine 2-1 victory.

Bo'ness played host to former Third Division side Lochgelly United. The plucky non-league team certainly made Bo'ness work for their victory, as they outplayed them for much of the first half, so much so that Bo'ness took half an hour to test keeper Paterson, much to the dismay of the home support. As their shouts were getting more frequent, this seemed to have an effect on Bo'ness, as just over a minute later they opened their account, Oswald the scorer. So desperate were Lochgelly to get on level terms that their centre forward almost hurled keeper Muir into the net as the pair went for a cross ball; Half time Bo'ness 1 Lochgelly United 0.

After the break, Bo'ness began to take charge with Burns, Gribbin and Martin all coming close to extending their lead. Lochgelly were certainly not out of the game, with Muir having to be at his best to save at the base of the post after good work from the left. With twenty minutes remaining, Gribbin was seriously hurt in a collision and had to leave the field of play. The game had just resumed when Burns met a cross from McGregor and scored an unexpected second goal for the home side. With Bo'ness now in a comfortable position, they began to knock the ball around confidently and just before the finish, Oswald grabbed his second and Bo'ness' third, to end with a flattering 3-0 score line.

The final match of the first round saw First Division Dunfermline Athletic visit Mill Park. Prior to the game Dunfermline lodged a protest against the eligibility of Bathgate's forward Gardener. On the morning of the game a letter from the SFA was received and the player was unable to play. This incident certainly added fire to the cup-tie as Bathgate had to make last minute alternations to their team. To make matters worse, Bathgate found themselves a goal down in less than ten minutes. However, this spurred the Mill Park players on and they proceeded to have the bulk of possession for the remainder of the half. They did manage to equalise on the half hour mark through Wilkie, but with many chances going a begging, they could easily have taken a commanding interval lead. Over-eagerness was probably one of the main reasons, as the home forwards were frequently being drawn up for offside.

Within two minutes of the restart, Bathgate took the lead after a Wales header found the net from fine play from Rutherford down the right wing. Bathgate then opted to defend their lead rather than to kill the game off, and this proved to be their downfall, as Dunfermline grabbed a hotly disputed equaliser with only six minutes remaining. Taylor only partially saved a Dunfermline effort, but Brown stepped in and attempted to clear off the line. Following a scrimmage, the referee ran in and immediately awarded a goal. Many of the Bathgate players vigorously protested against the decision, but after consulting his two linesmen, the referee remained adamant. Bathgate put the visitors under pressure for the remaining minutes and although creating a few chances, the game remained Bathgate 2 Dunfermline Athletic 2.

The replay the following Wednesday resulted in a 5-2 victory for Dunfermline, but the result as it looks on paper was anything but convincing, as Bathgate put up a great fight and it was in more ways down to their misfortune than the superiority of the home side. Fighting against a strong wind, Bathgate surprised their host by taking the lead just over the fifteen minute mark, with a well worked goal. A second could have been scored minutes later as Kennedy's shot was fumbled by the Fifer's keeper, who watched on as the ball slid past the wrong side of the post. Even after the homesters had equalised, Bathgate's defence stood up well to the onslaught of their opponents, who were taking full advantage of the wind. It appeared as if Bathgate would hold on till the interval, but a disastrous closing five minutes had Bathgate reeling, with a second goal for the Fifers, followed by a disputed third. Bathgate's keeper Taylor lying badly injured after he appeared to have been fouled, left Dunfermline forward Stein the easy task of heading home. This put a completely different complexion on the game, and although Taylor did appear for the second half, he looked anything but fit. To make matters worse, Bathgate defender McKinlay was also in the wars, and he too never fully recovered from his injury. If that was not bad enough, the strong wind that the visitors struggled against for forty-five minutes had more or less completely veered round. This meant that Bathgate had the unusual experience of having to counter the troublesome and by no means light breeze, for the entire ninety minutes. A fourth goal for the Pars ended any slim hopes of a comeback, even though Bathgate did manage a second; the First Division side wrapped it up with a fifth and final goal.

The second round draw was favourable to the County clubs, with Bo'ness and Broxburn both receiving home ties. Bo'ness got the chance to pit their wits against First Division opposition in the shape of Cowdenbeath, who at that time had pretty much established themselves as one of the high-flyers in the top division. Talking of which, Bo'ness were going great guns in the Second Division and were soon to be joining Cowdenbeath in top flight football, as within a few months, they would be crowned Second Division Champions.

From a Bo'ness standpoint, the start of their game was far from promising, as it became obvious that the importance of the occasion was affecting several of the players, who in the early stages were none too convincing. Still as a whole the team never allowed Cowdenbeath to dominate the situation, and with the defence standing up to its job, the period of anxiety was quickly diminishing.

By the time the first fifteen minutes had passed, Bo'ness were delivering blow for blow. Both teams passed up good opportunities to open their accounts, as this entertaining game swung from end to end. Eventually seven minutes from the interval Bo'ness opened the scoring. Martin found himself in a good position but was fouled just outside the box. Cottingham took the resulting free kick and a terrific drive left Cowdenbeath's keeper helpless. With the crowd now firmly behind the Homesters, Martin was unlucky not to add a second but his header was this time well saved by Falconer. Half-time Bo'ness 1 Cowdenbeath 0.

The second half started with both teams creating chances, with Martin in particular giving the visiting defence a hard time. The Bo'ness forward did have the ball in the net, but the referee awarded a foul, much to the relief of Fifers keeper, who had looked well beaten. This seemed to prompt Cowdenbeath into action, and on the hour mark Bo'ness failed to clear a corner resulting in the unmarked Wilson driving home the equaliser. Although Cowdenbeath's goal was against the run of play, it did not downhearten Bo'ness, who immediately proceeded to restore the lead. Within three minutes their efforts were rewarded, McGregor being largely instrumental in the scoring of the well deserved goal, as it was from his run and cross that Oswald nodded the ball into the net. The excitement was not intense as Cowdenbeath battled away for an equaliser, but Bo'ness matched their First Division opponents in every area and up until the final whistle, created the better chances and could easily have won by a larger margin. Nevertheless, it was a well merited victory, which saw the First Division team out-fought in every department.

Broxburn United welcomed the visit of Montrose at Sports Park, when a crowd of around 2,000 witnessed a 2-2 draw. With Broxburn taking advantage of shooting downhill, it was not until midway through the half that Reid opened the scoring. Up until then the Montrose defence had stayed firm and continued to do so up until the interval, as Broxburn failed to add to their tally. Into the second half, and a penalty kick put the visitors on level terms after McBurnie had handled in the area. A second penalty was awarded this time to Broxburn, again for handball, but Reid's effort was well saved by the keeper. Fortunately for the striker the keeper's clearance was anticipated by Reid, who cleverly drove the ball home well out of the keepers reach. In the closing minutes just as Broxburn had appeared to have won the tie, the visitors struck with an excellent drive that gave Bruce no chance. In the final minutes Montrose set up chance after chance, and could easily have stole the tie, but fortunately Bruce kept his cool, making several good saves.

Broxburn made a few changes for their visit to Links Park, notably Johnstone, a last minute signing from Heart of Midlothian. The visitors couldn't have got off to a worse start as Montrose took the lead within two minutes, following a well placed corner. Broxburn had the better of the match thereafter, but failed to open their account. Either side of half-time Broxburn came close to scoring, first up being new signing Johnstone, who saw a low drive come off the post. Rayne did likewise with a terrific effort. As the game advanced, the home defence stood firm and remained solid up until the final whistle, to earn themselves a third round visit to Tannadice.

Left down to Bo'ness, the third round draw was a little unkind, travel wise at least, as the West Lothian side had to make the long trek to Buckie. A special train left Bo'ness at 7.00am carrying two hundred passengers, which included the players, officials and supporters. On arrival the Bo'ness contingent were given a real Highland welcome, from the pipe band of the Gordon Highlanders, who were parading the pitch watched by over 4,000 spectators. Bo'ness opened strongly, with Martin opening the scoring on the fifteen minute mark. The same player had a couple of chances to increase their lead, but failed to hit the target on both occasions. Half-time Buckie 0 Bo'ness 1.

The Second Division leaders continued to have the bulk of the play and there was no doubt the West Lothian club's experience proved too much for Buckie, that and also poor finishing cost the home side dearly. It was not until the eightieth minute however, that Bo'ness wrapped up the tie, with Gribbin the scorer, when a few minutes from time, Oswald added a third and final goal.

The fourth round draw was made, and Celtic (then Scottish Champions) were to visit Bo'ness. Preparations were quickly made to house a record crowd. The directors of the club showed commendable enterprise by launching a scheme for the extension and improving of the terracing, plus additional turnstiles. Newtown Park was set to accommodate double its capacity, which came in at around 25,000. All this time and money however turned out to be a needless exercise, as the thousands of Celtic fans that were envisaged, failed to materialise and as the game kicked off, fewer than 10,000 supporters had turned up. The ten special trains that drew in to the Bo'ness station were relatively quiet; seven from Glasgow, with one each from Bathgate, Stirling and Lanark. Only the Bathgate train was worthy of a mention, packed out with well wishers from other parts of the county, loyally lending their support to the home side. With Rangers playing a short distance away at Falkirk, brake clubs from Glasgow were out in force, with Rangers supporters travelling via Cumbernauld, while the Celtic contingent travelled via Airdrie and Armadale. The rather less fortunate Celtic supporters, who had set off the previous night on foot, had to endure the most atrocious conditions, as heavy rain fell through the night.

Unfortunately the weather did not let up and the rain continued throughout the day. Celtic, taking no chances, were at full strength, while Bo'ness on the other hand were forced to make changes. These saw left winger McGregor being replaced by Heart of Midlothian's Smith, who slotted into the outside right position, while Oswald took up his favoured left wing position. The line up was as follows;

Bo'ness:- Muir, Young, Ramsey, falconer, Walker, Thomson, Smith, Gribbin, Martin, Cottingham and Oswald.
Celtic: - Thomson, W. McStay, Hilley, Wilson, J McStay, MacFarlane, Connolly, Thomson, McGlory, McInally and McLean.

Bo'ness took to the field sporting brand new strips (they were in fact borrowed from Lochmill FC Linlithgow, for the afternoon) and were greeted by a rousing reception, followed by Celtic who were also welcomed by loud applause. No time was wasted as Bo'ness kicked off six minutes before the scheduled time. End to end play characterised the opening exchanges, and up until the first fifteen minutes it seemed only a matter of time before the first goal would be scored. Sure enough the opener did arrive in the sixteenth minute, but totally against the run of play, McLean netting for the visitors after fine work from McGlory. As the game settled, both teams created chances, Smith in particular being unlucky not to have Bo'ness on level terms as he drove the ball from an acute angle, which skimmed the crossbar with Thomson well beaten. Other chances were made available to the normally efficient Cottingham, but much to the disappointment of the home support, the forward was having a rare off-day.

Just before the half-time whistle sounded, Thomson netted a second goal for the Parkhead side, after Muir failed to hold a McInally effort. To find themselves trailing by two goals at the interval was very unfortunate, but the second half was a different story. Within twenty minutes of the restart, Celtic were in triumphant form putting the 'Blues defence through a gruelling time. First up was McGlory in the fifty second minute, to put the tie beyond doubt, followed by a McInally effort two minutes later. McGlory added his second and Celtic's fifth, after which the visitors eased off. Late in the game Martin pulled one back, tapping in from close range, which was quickly followed up by a second goal, this time from Oswald. Nothing more than consolation goals, if anything, it did put a fairer reflection on the game. Bo'ness were out of the cup, their league campaign was a different story, as they were crowned Second Division champions, enabling them to have another crack at their Glasgow rivals.

THE BIGGER PICTURE

Falkirk went down 1-0 to Celtic at Ibrox after previously knocking out Rangers. Second Division East Fife shocked First Division Partick Thistle with a 2-1 victory at Tynecastle. However, Celtic proved too much for their lower league opponents, with a 3-1 win at Hampden Park.

The Scottish Cup for season 1927/28 saw only three West Lothian sides enter the competition, with Broxburn United stepping down to Junior status. This was to turn out a disappointing campaign for the remaining seniors, not one making it by the second round. With Bo'ness now in the top league, they travelled down to Somerset Park to take on Ayr United. Just like the previous season, which saw Bo'ness romp away with the Second Division title, Ayr were doing likewise, which in turn made it such a difficult trip down to the Ayrshire coast. A healthy crowd of around 11,000 gathered, with 400 of them travelling from Bo'ness.

The game started at a fast and furious pace with Ayr kicking off, but Bo'ness having two long range efforts just going wide of the target. Ayr's forward Smith replied with a double to give Ayr a two goal lead all within five minutes. Bo'ness almost pulled one back immediately when a Lynas drive shook the crossbar. Bo'ness continued to dominate huge spells of the match, but couldn't find that killer touch in front of goal. Bo'ness' luck totally deserted them when Oswald, their best player on the park, went off injured following a clash with Robertson, although he did manage to come back on near the end, the forward was limping badly. Despite their handicap, the 'Blues kept pegging away till the end but they failed to open their account.

For the second successive season Celtic were drawn away to a West Lothian club, but unlike their Bo'ness counterparts, the Bathgate directors decided to give away home advantage for a financial gain. With heavy rain and gusty winds, the horrendous weather conditions certainly affected the crowd, as little more than 3,000 spectators attended, with gate money adding up to little more than £150, this turned out to be Celtic's lowest

Scottish Cup attendance at Parkhead post WW1. On the plus side Celtic must have been impressed with Bathgate's Parker and Hughes, as they signed both players, in turn giving a much needed cash boost to the West Lothian club.

Bathgate: *Taylor, Clark, Bolton, frame, Westwood, Pearson, Higgins, Henderson, O'Hare, Parker and Hughes.*

Celtic: *J Thomson, W McStay, McGonnigle, Wilson, J McStay, Doyle, Connolly, A Thompson, McGrory, McInally and McLean.*

Bathgate did not succeed in causing a sensation at Parkhead, but it has to be said that their display was something of a revelation even to their own supporters. Even though Celtic were indisputably the more polished side throughout, they were fully stretched to enter into the next round of the competition. To go down 3-1 was anything but a humbling result from the Bathgate point of view. Bathgate started well and thought they had taken an early lead, only for the referee to call for offside. Then after fourteen minutes Celtic's McLean was yards offside as he lobbed the ball towards goal. McGrory harassed Taylor as he was about to save and the ball trundled into the net. Ten minutes before the interval Celtic increased their lead once again, with McLean finding the net tapping home after his first effort struck the post. Bathgate never gave up the fight and before halftime a fine cross from Higgins found Parker, who was running in on goal, slammed the ball into the net. The second half was evenly balanced with Parker, Henderson and Higgins all having shots at goal, at the other end Taylor was in fine form to save splendidly from McGrory. With fifteen minutes remaining, McInally sealed the game for Celtic, with a third and final goal. In the light of Bathgate's plucky show, many of the clubs supporters were left wondering what could have happened if the match had remained at Mill Park.

The final match of the first round saw Armadale entertain Berwick Rangers at the Volunteer Park. Again horrendous weather conditions ruined the game as heavy rain fell throughout the ninety minutes. Armadale adjusted quicker to the waterlogged surface and the fierce gale by opening their account with little more than five minutes on the clock, following a cross by Hunter. Martin in turn sent it over to Love, who smashed the ball into the net in off the bar. Armadale continued to have the bulk of the match, but after twenty-five minutes, a bizarre incident occurred. Berwick's striker Reeves picking the ball up in the penalty area unleashed a drive which found the back of the net. The ball then however struck a post behind the goal before spinning towards the corner flag. As Reeves was being congratulated by his team mates, the referee inspected the goal nets before coming to the conclusion that the ball had gone by the outside of the post then proceeded in awarding a goal kick. Berwick were not to be outdone however, and within a minute Reeves beat King with an unstoppable drive. That goal prompted Armadale into action as they lay siege on the visitors goal, a Wardrope header which slammed off the crossbar was the nearest they came before the interval.

Into the second half and the 'Dale continued to dominate proceedings, putting the Berwick defence under intense pressure. The home support however, had to wait until midway through the second half before Love added a second with an overhead kick. Wardrope added a third and final goal late on to secure Armadale a place in the second round.

With Armadale being West Lothian's last hopes in the competition, the match bought out the largest crowd of the season to the Volunteer Park. This was helped on by a sizably contingent from Stirling, which consisted of a special train and fifteen buses to cheer on Kings Park. Throughout the week a heavy snowfall covered the pitch, but through the efforts of a large number of enthusiasts, this was cleared on time. Unfortunately heavy rain once again fell prior to kick off, making an already soft pitch worse. Bo'ness did the neighbourly thing releasing both Creighton and Duff to Armadale on loan deals. The Armadale line-up was as follows; *King, Tonner, Creighton, Calderwood, Muir, Duff, Hunter, Love, Wardrope, Polland and Grove.*

Kings Park did all the early running, but slowly the home side came into the match, and with only eight minutes till the interval on loan signing Duff opened the scoring. Following a corner, the Bo'ness player shot in the direction of goal and was probably the most astonished player on the field as he saw the ball reach the net through a crowd of players. Within five minutes however, Kings Park were on level terms. Shortly into the second half Kings Park were awarded a penalty which they duly converted. Armadale were then given a perfect opportunity to equalise as they too were awarded a spot kick, but the normally trusted Wardrope shot past the post much to the dismay of the home support. Success was not long delayed however, as Grove headed home following a corner. This inspired Armadale and a fast flowing attack involving four players saw Hunter's final effort go out for a corner. The resulting corner was cleared, which saw Kings Park go up the other end of the field and regain the lead. Armadale players gave their all in search of an equaliser, but the tiring home side went further being in the last minute, when goalkeeper King miss-hit a clearance, leaving Kings Park's Toner the simple task of tapping into the empty net. Final Score: Armadale 2 Kings Park 4.

THE BIGGER PICTURE

Celtic travelled to Ibrox and recorded a 2-1 victory over Queens Park, Rangers set up an Old Firm final defeating Hibernian 3-0 at Tynecastle. A record crowd of 118,115 saw no fewer than eighteen internationals take the field, after a goal-less first half, Rangers ended up easy winners with a 4-0 victory.

All three teams, Armadale, Bathgate and Bo'ness cruised into the second round of the cup but it has to be said against mediocre opposition.

A crowd of around 650 watched on at the Recreation Park, St. Andrews, as the University students took on Bathgate. In a match that was totally dominated by Bathgate, it was somewhat surprising that it took the visitors twenty-five minutes to open their account, with Tallis scoring from close range. It was not until a few minutes before the interval that Bathgate managed to breach the stubborn home defence, this time Fairley hitting the net with a powerful drive. During the second half Bathgate took their foot off the pedal, but were never in any danger of losing. All the applause had to go to the Universities keeper Wann, who certainly kept the scoreline respectable, he could do nothing however to stop Tallis grabbing his second, and Bathgate's third in the dying minutes.

Newton Stewart visited Newtown Park and once again a comfortable victory was achieved by Bo'ness. The West Lothian side took the game in hand right away and sealed the victory within the first half hour with four goals, with Clark and Haggerty scoring two a piece. Three further second half goals from Ross, Russell and a final late goal for Clark to secure his hat-trick made it an easy afternoon for the 'Blues. Newton Stewart did manage to score a consolation, but it was all down to good goalkeeping and the woodwork that kept the game in single figures, in the end a satisfactory win. Final Score: Bo'ness 7 Newton Stewart 1.

Armadale recorded the highest win of the afternoon with an easy victory over Renfrewshire Amateur side Moorpark at the Volunteer Park. The visitors started lively enough but it was to be Armadale who were to open their account after fifteen minutes, Heigh the scorer. Moorpark were a little unfortunate when they lost the services of one of their backs on the half hour mark. Down to ten men they immediately lost a second goal, Young applying the finishing touch. With no further scoring in the first half, Armadale came out all guns blazing, and within fifteen minutes of the second half, Young had grabbed his hat-trick, while Heigh had notched his second. Soon after Moorpark surprised the homesters by pulling a goal back. Armadale should have regained their five goal advantage soon after, as Lawrie's penalty kick came back off the post, he latched on to the rebound and netted, but of course the goal was disallowed. Armadale had the upper hand, and it was no surprise to see Polland firing in number six. Once again Moorpark pulled one back only for Douglas to net number seven. Moorpark blasted a penalty over the bar before Heigh doubled his tally to four in the closing stages to round off a satisfying 9-2 victory. All three County teams were drawn against First Division opposition in the second round of the tournament, with only Bathgate receiving a home tie, the remaining pair making the trip down the west coast to take on Ayrshire opposition.

First up was Armadale who travelled to Somerset Park to take on Ayr United. In a first half that was mainly dominated by the home side, Armadale surprised their hosts by taking a half time lead, the goal coming in the thirty-eighth minute. As the Ayr keeper was in the process of clearing the ball, Young nipped in and kicked the ball out of his hand and into the net. The goal was certainly underserved on play, but there was no mistaking the eagerness of the Armadale team. The second half and Ayr came out in determined fashion, and within six minutes were on level terms. It was not until midway through the half that Ayr eventually took the lead, the 'Dale ought to have levelled a minute later, Young miss-kicking in front of an open goal, and soon after Heigh was unlucky with a header. As the game wore on, United took control of the game and added a further three late goals to finish with a deserved 5-1 victory.

110

Bo'ness visited neighbouring Kilmarnock and were well received as a large following had travelled to lend their support. It must have been satisfying for them to see their former goal scorer Chris Martin making an appearance on loan from Falkirk, along with Good of Raith Rovers. In one of the hardest games seen at Rugby Park that season, the match was fought out in typical cup tie fashion. Bo'ness, however, couldn't have got off to a worse start as they fell behind with only two minutes played. Far from disheartened, Bo'ness rallied on and deservedly equalised, after some fine work from Ross and Martin, and Fleming cleverly applied the finishing touch. The jubilation from their followers was short lived however, as Kilmarnock regained the lead within a couple of minutes. Up until the half time whistle, play had somewhat quietened down, with both defences having little to do. Bo'ness started brightly in the second half, within a few minutes Fleming grabbed his second to put Bo'ness on level terms. As in the opening period, Kilmarnock speedily restored their lead. Bo'ness continued to hold their own and never lost sight of forcing a replay. In one attack, they came close to equalising as the ball came back off the post with the keeper beaten, but sadly that was as close as it got. In what was an exciting game, Kilmarnock just doing enough to see off the battling Bo'ness side.

The final match of the second round saw a home tie for Bathgate as they took on Raith Rovers at Mill Park. A reasonable crowd gathered for the game which peaked around the 3,000 mark, which included several hundred from Kirkcaldy. The game was barely two minutes old when Bathgate found themselves trailing one goal behind to the First Division side. In a lively match both teams were in all out attack with possibly Bathgate being a little unlucky not to be on level terms at the interval. Nothing daunted the Mill Park players, who attacked determinedly and equalised within five minutes of the second half, Drummond on hand to sweep the ball into the corner of the net. The game continued at an arousing pace until the close, with both teams creating chances to win.

The replay on the Wednesday once again saw Raith Rovers take an early lead, Bruton scoring in the first minute, and after a few unsuccessful efforts from Bathgate, Bruton scored his second. Rovers eased off somewhat allowing Bathgate back into the game, but good defending on several occasions from the home defence prevented any scoring. Eventually just before half time, Bathgate's Fairly managed to reduce the leeway. On resuming Bathgate went all out in attack and Drummond quickly levelled the scores. A minute later McPherson forced a brilliant save from the home keeper. Bathgate were now playing every bit as good as their opponents, but a misunderstanding lead to their downfall. While the Mill Park defence stood appealing for off-side, Bruton nipped in to seal his hat-trick, a minute later he scored his fourth. Before the finish he was brought down in the box by Westwood, and from the spot kick he beat Dempster to round off the scoring. In the end an easy win for Raith Rovers, but Bathgate certainly made a game of it.

THE BIGGER PICTURE

Kilmarnock first of all beat Celtic 1-0 at Ibrox, then Rangers 2-0 at Hampden Park to lift the Scottish Cup for the second time. Rangers had defeated St. Mirren 3-2 in the other semi-final.

1929-30 season saw the return of the Scottish Qualifying Cup, the reason being Bathgate FC were no longer a Scottish League Club. Nearing the end of the previous season Bathgate resigned with eight games remaining, financial restraints were too much for the club, similar to Broxburn's problems a few years earlier, and they too joined the non-league option and went back to amateur status, where the money side of matters were less severe.

As it turned out the competition proved just as successful as ten years previously, as Bathgate went on to lift the trophy for a second time with victories over Peebles Rovers, Duns, Murrayfield Amateurs, Vale of Leithen, Civil Service Strollers and finally Inverness Citadel. This set them up nicely for the final against St. Cuthbert's Wanderers at Palmerston Park in Dumfries. A crowd of 3,650 gathered in what can only be described as appalling conditions, as the weather was stormy and rain fell throughout the ninety minutes of play, which in turn made it very unpleasant for the players and spectators alike. Bathgate having the better of the first half, went in at the interval leading by a tenth minute Somerville goal. The second half saw St. Cuthbert's play with a lot more determination but failed to break down the maroon's defence. At the end of the day that one first half goal was enough to see the trophy head back to Bathgate. Arriving home a crowd of over a thousand gave the Bathgate team a great reception at Bathgate Upper Station. Team Captain Gavin Kerr was carried shoulder high holding the cup aloft as they weaved through the streets to the Commercial Hotel, where a final speech was made by Mr Hardy, the club president.

This victory lead Bathgate to a first round tie away from home against Second Division King's Park. The Bathgate team were as follows: - Greenhorn, Walker, Jamieson, Keir, Curie, Baird, Frew, McAllister, Dick, Welsh and Somerville.

The Stirling side proved too much of a handful as they swept Bathgate aside, taking the lead within three minutes, they added a further three before the interval. Dick also scored for Bathgate in the first forty five, but at that stage the match was finished as a contest. Midway through the second half, Dick managed to reduce the lee-way with a second goal, but Kings Park regained their three goal advantage a few minutes later. Five minutes from the final whistle, the Stirling side rounded off the scoring, final result Kings Park 6 Bathgate 2.

Armadale travelled north to take on Inverness Citadel. This game had been brought forward to the Wednesday, and Armadale wanted a £60 guarantee, while Citadel offered £45, it looked like the game would have to be switched to the original date, but late on, Armadale accepted the smaller sum. Also fixed up in the last minute was ex-Airdrieonian inside left John Allison. In the end all was in vain as the 'Dale went down 1-0 to the Highland League outfit.

The final tie of the round saw Bo'ness entertain St. Johnstone. A stuffy display by the Bo'ness rearguard kept their First Division opponents at bay, although both teams had chances to score, Bo'ness probably the more likely. Clark was most unlucky with a powerful shot that came off the underside of the bar, with the Saints keeper well beaten. The replay up in Perth saw a lack lustre performance from the West Lothian side as they went down 3-1.

THE BIGGER PICTURE

With Partick Thistle defeating Hamilton 3-1 at Celtic Park and Rangers comfortably winning 4-1 at Hampden Park against Heart of Midlothian, everything was on the line for a repeat shock of the 1921 cup final. Although Partick put up a good fight, their name never went on the trophy as they went down 2-1 after a 0-0 draw.

1930-31 season saw Bathgate FC retain the Scottish Qualifying Cup, with victories over Coldstream, Leith Amateurs, Peebles Rovers, Civil Service Strollers, Falkirk Amateurs and Buckie Thistle set them up against Dalbeattie Star. After a 1-1 draw at Palmerston Park, the replay was held at Somerset Park in Ayr, which saw Bathgate do just enough to win the trophy. The winning line-up was as follows:-J. Greenhorn, J. Gordon, A Jamieson, G Kerr, W. Currie, R. Smith, J. Frew, D. McAllister, T. Dick, J. Walker and P. Somerville.

A suspicious looking off-side goal near the end of the first half from Dick was all that separated the sides. Bathgate created several chances in the second half to clinch the trophy, but it took sterling work from the Bathgate defence late on to save the West Lothian side, where a replay might have been necessary. The team, just like the year before, received a warm reception as they arrived at the station, and once again the team captain was lifted shoulder high carrying the Qualifying Cup. Around 1,000 supporters gathered in and around the steelyard as the crowd passed by towards the Commercial Hotel.

All Bathgate's hard work was duly rewarded with a trip to Fir Park to take on a Motherwell side which was going through the best period in their history.
The attendance was disappointing, despite the fine weather, it amounted to just over 2,500. Bathgate fielded the eleven that won the Qualifying Cup with one exception, W. Ramsey their latest acquisition from Fauldhouse Bluebell replacing G. Kerr. With less than three minutes on the clock Motherwell took the lead, the home side continued to dominate throughout the first half but Bathgate stood firm, with Greenhorn saving the visitors on numerous occasions. The keeper was having the game of his life and even saved a penalty after new signing Ramsey fouled in the box. As the half time whistle sounded Greenhorn was applauded off the park.

114

Motherwell resumed on the offensive, but Greenhorn was not to be beaten as he pulled off save after save. Eventually on the hour mark, Motherwell's Stevenson scored the first of his four goals, the home side eventually cruised home to a 6-0 victory, but the keeper was not at fault with any of the goals. When the final whistle sounded, the keeper received an even greater ovation than he received at the interval. One Motherwell supporter was heard to remark that the great display from Greenhorn was worth the admission fee alone.

Match of the day in the County was undoubtedly the tie at Volunteer Park where Armadale took on the cup holders Rangers. Leading up to the match Armadale Directors wasted no time preparing for the match, on the pitch four new signings were made, off the park, crush barriers were erected along with additional turnstiles. All set and Saturday arrived, the crowd gathered quickly and an hour before the start there was several thousand inside the ground, with the new turnstiles clicking away merrily, there seemed indications that there would be a record attendance, but the expected rush did not materialise. The official attendance coming in at 8,800, of that a large following travelling from Glasgow. Armadale were first to take the field looking smart in their new strips of white shirts with black shorts and were given a rousing reception. Rangers followed a minute or so later, and it was at once apparent that they would lack nothing the way of vocal support. The teams were as follows: - *Armadale: Watson, Findlay, Hamilton, Joseph Polland, Fyfe, Hailstones, Fleming, Stout, Brannan, Livingston and John Polland. Rangers: T Hamilton, Gray, R Hamilton, McDonald, Simpson, Buchanan, Archibald, Marshall, Fleming, McPhail and Morton.*

All the hype leading up to this match was soon to disappear after only fifteen minutes play, McPhail was boring down on goal when he was brought down by Hamilton. On regaining his feet he assumed a threatening attitude towards the player but the referee promptly intervened. It created a general surprise however, when the official ordered Hamilton off the field, with seventy-five minutes still to play, he robbed the game of any real interest and any hopes of a shock result were over. It took Rangers just over the half hour mark to open their account, Fleming the scorer. Within two minutes the visitors were two ahead, this time around Morton scoring from the spot. Although Armadale battled away bravely and created a few chances, they were at too much of a disadvantage and it was no surprise to see them going further behind eight minutes before the interval, as McPhail added a third.

Twelve minutes after the break and Fleming added a fourth, and within five minutes McPhail grabbed his second. Armadale's fighting spirit was still evident and when the Rangers keeper spilled a Livingstone effort, Brannan was on hand to bang the ball into the net. Eight minutes from the end and Marshall added a sixth, with a couple of minutes later Fleming getting his hat-trick scoring from close range. This rounded off the scoring in a game which was disappointing in many respects. Result: Armadale 1 Rangers 7.

Finally Bo'ness entertained Highland League side Peterhead at Newtown Park. 1,200 spectators witnessed a gallant fight from the northeast side, which on a few occasions were desperately unlucky not to take the lead. Bo'ness, with the lion's share of possession, struggled to find any rhythm, and it was not until twenty minutes from the end that Taylor eventually broke the deadlock, which was quickly followed up by a second goal from Aitken. With a two goal lead, Bo'ness were a totally different team, and the pace had now been eased considerably. Bo'ness seemed quite content with their lead and Peterhead appearing reconciled to defeat. In the closing minutes Taylor wrapped the tie up with his second and Bo'ness' third. Result: Bo'ness 3 Peterhead 0.

The second round tie between Bo'ness and Alloa took two attempts, due to severe weather conditions. There was a thin covering of snow on the pitch when the game began in front of 500 spectators. Both teams put on a creditable show as they battled against an unbearable wind and driving sleet, and the pitch which had turned into a quagmire. It was to be no surprise therefore when five minutes before the interval, Anderson the Bo'ness winger collapsed from exposure. The referee held a hurried consultation and decided to abandon the game. Under the circumstances it was a wise decision as there was no doubt if the match had continued further casualties would have come about. After forty minutes play, the game stood level at 0-0.

The replay took place the following Wednesday afternoon when the weather was fair, with an attendance of around 1,000 watching the game, which began at a frantic pace with both teams creating numerous chances.

116

Bo'ness, at this stage being the better of the teams, took the lead after clever work from McLaren and Lumsden, the ball was swung over to Taylor, who headed into the net. Within a couple of minutes Alloa were level. From a Bo'ness point of view it was a soft goal to lose. Bo'ness contained to have the upper hand and before the interval Taylor restored the lead with another headed goal. On the resumption Alloa quickly levelled the scores, and the game continued at a frantic pace with heavy tackles coming in from both teams. A Pratt goal again gave the home team the advantage, soon after Taylor was forced to retire due to injury. For the final ten minutes or so Bo'ness struggled on with ten men; however Lumsden added a fourth and final goal in the closing minutes to make sure of victory.

Bo'ness got the luck of the draw with a home tie against First Division strugglers Ayr United. Bo'ness too had their problems as they sat rooted to the bottom of the Second Division, a position they were to find themselves till the end of the season. Nevertheless they continued to impress on Scottish Cup duty and deservedly booked their place into the last eight with a hard fought but worthy victory over their First Division rivals. With the match heading for a goal-less draw, Bo'ness had a strong penalty claim turned down, despite repeated appeals from the Bo'ness players, the referee refused to grant any award. Feelings were now shown from players and spectators alike as Bo'ness drove forward in determined fashion, when a foul was committed just outside the box. McLaren took the resulting free kick and found McDonald who headed into the net with only five minutes remaining. Ayr tried desperately to force a replay, but the home defence stood solid for a memorable win.

Once again home advantage for Bo'ness was given, against a strong mid table First Division side in the shape of Kilmarnock, a team which had won the trophy a few years earlier. Taking this into account, and the fact that a place in the semi-finals was only ninety minutes away, a crowd of over 6,000 gathered for Newton Park's best attendance for a good few seasons. The Bo'ness team that day was as follows: - *Fraser, Clark, Gray, W. Aitken, Davis, McLaren, Lumsden, J Aitken, Taylor, Heeps and Pratt.*

There was to be mixed fortunes for Bo'ness at the beginning of the match; with only a few minutes played W. Aitken went off injured. Even with ten men there was no holding Bo'ness, and an attack down the right resulted in a free kick just outside the box, which was in turn floated over by J. Aitken, where Pratt was on hand to head home the opening goal after just six minutes. W. Aitken returned limping badly, and with this handicap Bo'ness were "put through the mill" as Kilmarnock desperately tried to find that equalising goal. With a now tired looking Bo'ness side, it looked as if they had weathered the storm and a semi-final place was only minutes away, Kilmarnock had other ideas however and in the final minute broke the hearts of the homesters with a last gasp goal. The goal was deserved on the run of play, yet it was hard luck on gallant Bo'ness who had struggled on gamely with practically ten men.

The match was nearly a cup tie shock as ever it could be, and had Bo'ness had the fully affective services of W. Aitken they would probably have won the tie. As it turned out Bo'ness travelled down to Rugby Park the following Wednesday and were a well beaten side. Kilmarnock took the lead after eight minutes and added a second before the interval. Tussles between Bo'ness' Lumsden and Kilmarnock's Nibloe had always been of the robust order with the result the players being at loggerheads. While the referee issued out a warning to Lumsden, J. Aitken argued the point with the referee, resulting in the Bo'ness man being sent to the pavilion, and what little chance Bo'ness had quickly disappeared. Kilmarnock added a third before Nibloe got his marching orders for a rash tackle on Lumsden who had to be carried off the pitch much to the disgust of the small band of travelling supporters. Kilmarnock added a further two goals before the end resulting in a comfortable 5-0 victory.

THE BIGGER PICTURE

Kilmarnock went down 3-0 to Celtic at Hampden, while Motherwell eased by St Mirren at Ibrox winning 1-0. A record gate of 131,273 watched a Motherwell side outplay Celtic and lead 2-0 with only ten minutes remaining, Celtic pulled one back before a own goal in the dying seconds tied the scores, in the replay Motherwell went down 4-2.

Holders Bathgate went down 3-1 to Leith Amateurs in the first round of the Qualifying Cup, this turned out to be Bathgate's last ever match in the National competition. It was now all down to Armadale and Bo'ness but things were far from rosy for both clubs as they too were struggling financially. Both teams however managed to progress past the first round. Armadale were given a home tie against Montrose, where an above average attendance of just over a thousand braved the stormy conditions as torrential rain swept through the county. Montrose winning the toss took advantage of the strong wind and took the lead with fifteen minutes on the clock but their lead was short lived however as Armadale's Weir equalised within five minutes after fine work from Johnstone. Five minutes after the interval Weir put Armadale ahead from the spot after a handball incident. It was not until the seventy-fifth minute however that the Armadale support could relax as Armadale scored a third goal, again the outcome of a penalty kick. Weir, who had been brought down, was entrusted with the kick which he duly took, completing his hat-trick and round off the scoring.

Bo'ness made the long trip south to take on Dalbeattie Star, where they had on show their latest singing Plenderleith from Preston North End. Weather conditions for the match seemed to be on par with West Lothian. Although starting brightly, Bo'ness found themselves two goals down as Star's early uncertainty disappeared as they took advantage of Bo'ness' shaky defence. With half-time approaching however, the 'Blues pulled one back from the penalty spot, Wallace converting the kick.

Resuming with the wind behind them, Bo'ness appeared a different team as they totally dominated the second half. Bo'ness keeper Simpson was more or less a spectator, where on the other hand the Dalbeattie keeper was in constant action. With less than fifteen minutes remaining, Bo'ness eventually got the goal they richly deserved, even if there was a little luck involved. A Carruthers corner was caught by the home keeper but he failed to hold, although he did manage to do so at the second attempt. After consulting with his linesman, the referee awarded a goal. With only a few minutes remaining, Carruthers waded through the Dalbeattie defence to grab his second and Bo'ness' third to clinch the tie.

Both clubs were rewarded with First Division opponents, Armadale travelled to Douglas Park to take on Hamilton Academicals, where a disappointing 3,000 crowd did little in monetary terms for the cash strapped West Lothian side, as the gate drawings added up to just over £80. In a rather one sided match, Armadale were scarcely seen on the attack, and by halftime Hamilton were coasting to victory leading 2-0. A penalty goal by Weir for Armadale seven minutes after the restart brought a little life into the game, but within six minutes Hamilton had restored their two goal advantage. Midway through the second half and Armadale's Weir sensationally reduced the leeway with a superbly struck shot. Armadale were now fighting hard for the equaliser, but all hopes were dashed when Hamilton struck a fourth with three minutes remaining. With the last kick of the ball Hamilton grabbed a fifth. The old phrase "beaten but not disgraced" would be fitting for Armadale's efforts and maybe if they had come out the hat first they would most certainly have given their Lanarkshire opponents a more torrid time at the Volunteer.

Bo'ness did get the luck of the draw which saw Partick Thistle journey to Newton Park. The attendance was over 6,000, which included over a thousand who paid via the unemployment gate. Among the crowd was a large contingent from Falkirk who had travelled out to see Partick's Evelyn Morrison, a former favourite for the Brockville Club.

Bo'ness maintained their reputation as cup fighters by holding their First Division opponents to a 2-2 draw. Bo'ness started well and deservedly took the lead on the half hour mark, with a well taken strike from Wallace. Five minutes after the interval Partick equalised with a disputed penalty after Stewart "innocently" handled in the area. To make matters worse, during the attack that led to a penalty, the visitors looked suspiciously offside. Encouraged by their success Thistle looked to have won the tie, when they added a second with fifteen minutes remaining. But with less than five minutes on the clock, Wallace equalised from the spot. From there on in Partick lay siege on the Bo'ness goal but the defence held off for a deserved draw. The replay at Firhill the following Wednesday saw Thistle run out easy 5-1 winners after a goal-less first half, Carruthers scoring Bo'ness' consolation. Finishing on a welcome note, Bo'ness took their share of the £470 from the 16,000 attendance.

THE BIGGER PICTURE

Kilmarnock beat Airdrieonians 3-2 at Firhill Park, while over at Celtic Park, Rangers saw off Hamilton Academicals 5-2. It took two games to decide the final, Rangers eventually winning 3-0 after a 1-1 draw.

120

The 1932-33 season was to spell the end to Scottish League football for both Armadale and Bo'ness. First to go was Bo'ness as they failed to pay guarantees to visiting clubs Brechin City and Stenhousemuir, and were expelled from the league. The Brechin City match was the final league game played on the 20th October 1932, when only 200 turned up to witness a 4-3 victory. Newcastle United offered to fulfil the remaining fixtures of the Newtown Park club, but their effort was knocked back. With dwindling crowds Armadale's fate was just around the corner. 300 spectators turned up for what was to be the last league game against Raith Rovers, three weeks after Bo'ness' expulsion on the 19th November 1932. Armadale could not make the £50 guarantee and also ended their membership to the Scottish League. On the 21st of January 1933, however, both clubs did manage to fill their Scottish Cup commitments. Armadale's home tie against Dundee United was watched by only 1,000 spectators. The Armadale directors spared no effort to put as strong a side as possible on the pitch, signing no fewer than four players, amongst those ex Celtic pair Pat Connelly and Tommy McInally. Armadale's last senior eleven was as follows;

Wilkinson, Boyle, Scott, Hamilton, Forrester, Fleming, Connelly, McInally, Michie, Miller and Imrie.

Despite the frostbound pitch being heavily sanded, Armadale settled well and gave a good account for a team that had not played a competitive match for two months. Armadale being the more aggressive side were a little unlucky when Michie seemed to have opened the scoring, but he was judged offside. As the game swung from end to end, both teams had chances but failed to open the scoring before the interval. After an encouraging start, Armadale found themselves a goal down just after the hour mark. Armadale never gave up as they pressed for the equaliser, but after a few near misses, United wrapped up the tie after a defensive slip-up from Scott with ten minutes remaining, not only bringing a close to Armadale's cup campaign, but also to their long senior history.

In order to put together a side for their visit to Stranraer, Bo'ness held a trials match the previous Saturday at Newtown Park, watched by over 700 spectators. The outcome of this match saw the following team take to the field at Stair Park;

Dudgeon (*Portsmouth*), Hogg (*Parkhead*), Gray, Bell, Burke (*Hibernian*), Fagan, McDonald (*Brighton & Hove Albion*), Whitters (*St. Mirren*), Main (*St. Johnstone*) Baxter (*Leicester*) and T. McDonald (*Armadale*).

The make-shift side managed to hold their own and earn a reply, Whitters scoring on the hour mark cancelling out Stranraer's opener after just five minutes. Although Stranraer had the bulk of the possession, Whitters was a constant threat to the Stranraer defence, while Dudgeon in goal coped well with everything the home side could throw at him. The keeper took some hefty knocks throughout the tie but managed to finish the game. The replay at Newtown saw both teams struggle to get to grips with the frost bound pitch, which in turn made it a dour struggle for the 1,700 or so that had gathered. Fully half an hour had gone before T. McDonald hammered the ball into the roof of the net, to put the 'Blues in front. This goal settled the home side down and play began to look that little more interesting. It was not until the second period when further goals from M. McDonald and Main put the tie beyond doubt to give Bo'ness a deserved win after their uninspiring start.

The second round saw Bo'ness travel to Dens Park on a Wednesday afternoon to avoid clashing with the Dundee United v St. Johnstone tie at Tannadice. Bo'ness after their many years in league football had the distinction of being the only non-league club left in the competition. With Dundee being a First Division outfit, the gap proved too much for Bo'ness as they went down 4-0. They did however manage to hold Dundee for most of the first half, at the same time creating a good few chances. They took advantage of a strong breeze before Dundee opened their account in the thirty-eighth minute. Eight minutes after the restart, Dundee doubled their lead and a further two goals from Balfour who had scored the first half goal secured his hat-trick to complete the scoring.

THE BIGGER PICTURE

Celtic knocked Hearts out at the second attempt winning 2-1, after a 0-0 draw, once again it was to be a Celtic v Motherwell final. A McGrory goal for Celtic was all that separated the sides, both teams each had seven survivors from the match two years earlier, Celtic had lost keeper John Thompson in tragic circumstances as he died after a collision in a match against Rangers.

122

The Scottish Qualifying Cup saw West Lothian's latest senior club make their debut in the competition. Broxburn St. John's as it happens, it was their only appearance, going down 7-1 to Vale of Leithen at the Sports Park. Armadale drawn to take on Civil Service Strollers by this time were finished and scratched to the Edinburgh club. Bo'ness travelled to Selkirk and went down 3-0, all the goals coming from Trantor in the first half. This turned out to be Selkirk's first success of reaching the second round of the competition since the end of the Great War. It also meant that West Lothian failed to have a representative in the national trophy since 1906-07 season.

THE BIGGER PICTURE

Motherwell and St. Mirren met at Tynecastle Park in which the Paisley club marched on to the final with a 3-1 win. The other semi-final at Hampden Park saw Rangers score the only goal of the game against St. Johnstone. The final was a different story however, as Rangers hammered five past St. Mirren without reply.

It was touch and go whether Bo'ness would have a team for the 1934-35 campaign. A meeting was held at the Unionist Hall to discuss if it was worthwhile having senior football in the town. In view of the meagre attendance, a pitiful thirty was certainly not an encouraging sign. In the end a vote was cast and Bo'ness would carry on. Drawn at home to Gala Fairydean in the Qualifying Cup, the clubs director's had two days to assemble a team. On paper at least the sensational team the management had found seemed a likely lot and made impressive reading;

Dudgeon (formerly Hibernian), Townsley (Falkirk, King (Heart of Midlothian), Brown (Millwall), Gallacher (Celtic), Sharkey (Hibernian), Duffy (Kings Park), Chalmers (Airdrieonians), Burt (Queen of the South), Davidson (Tottenham Hotspur) and Picken (Broxburn Shamrock).

A few of the players had previously played for Bo'ness, but for the others it seemed they had seen their better days. Never the less a 1200 spectators gathered for the match, which wasn't too bad considering the big local derby between Bo'ness Cadora and Linlithgow Rose was also being played in the town (5-1 to Cadora). On the day Bo'ness were too strong for the

123

Borders club with Chalmers, Burt and Duffy all scoring in a satisfactory 3-0 win. Victories over Berwick Rangers and Peebles Rovers saw Bo'ness make their second final appearance in the competition. The final played at Somerset Park saw Beith deservedly lift the trophy with a 2-1 win after a 1-1 draw. Fewer than 4,000 spectators witnessed both games.

When the first round draw for the Scottish Cup was made, the older Bo'ness supporters must have cast their minds back to the last visit to Cappielow Park on Scottish Cup duty, which saw the home side run riot banging in ten goals without reply. The only consolation this Bo'ness side could take out of the game was that they fared slightly better than their previous counterparts, but only just. Once again Morton totally outclassed their non-league opponents, this time to the tune of 9-0.

THE BIGGER PICTURE

Hamilton made their second cup final appearance after knocking out Aberdeen at Celtic Park by a 2-1 scoreline. The other semi-final, Rangers saw off Hearts 2-0 at Hampden after a 1-1 draw. Rangers edged by with a 2-1 victory to retain the trophy.

Bo'ness' best football was once again found in the Qualifying Cup competition, which brought about another final appearance. Victories over Vale of Leithen, Penicuik, Chinside United and Peebles Rovers set them up against Ayrshire side Galston. With the final being played on their doorstep at Brockville Park, everything seemed in place to win the trophy, after having two disappointing finals in the past. Sadly it did not prove third time lucky, as Galston coasted to a 4-0 victory. After losing two early goals the first within five minutes, followed by a second fifteen minutes later, it was always going to be an uphill struggle. Bo'ness did have the bulk of possession for the remainder of the half, but the damage had already been done. In the sixty-eighth minute Galston wrapped the game up with a third, after a Dudgeon error and within two minutes added a fourth. The concluding stages were fought out with Bo'ness struggling valiantly to prevent further disaster.

The first round of the Scottish Cup saw Airdrieonians visit Newtown Park. The Lanarkshire side tried to get the match switched to Broomfield, but Bo'ness refused the invitation based on the view that the lack of senior

124

football in the county would be affected, even though the chance came but once a year. With the pitch unplayable due to snow and ice, the match commenced the following week, watched by over 2,000, with a large contingent accompanying the Lanarkshire outfit. Before the start the teams lined up in the middle of the park as a two minutes silence was observed in memory of the late King. Airdrie took the lead after nine minutes with a shot that went in off the post, rebounding past the outstretched hand of keeper Miller, Bo'ness' most recent signing. After losing that rather lucky goal, Bo'ness soon recovered from their early attack of nerves and pressed confidently forward. Play was inclined to be scrappy with the referee constantly dishing out free kicks. However, after thirty minutes play, Bo'ness sensationally equalised with Cowan smashing the ball home with a twenty yard drive, hitting the upright on its way into the net. Bo'ness were unlucky not to take the lead when Cowan and Paterson just failed to squeeze the ball home following a free kick. Before the half time whistle, Airdrie regained their lead when Law shot past the unsighted Miller in goal. The second half saw both teams create a number of chances and in the sixty-fifth minute Airdrie took one of theirs when Law (ex-Bo'ness player) wrapped the game up and finish the scoring at 3-1. All in all the Combination League side put up a surprisingly good show against the First Division strugglers and with a little luck could easily have forced a replay.

THE BIGGER PICTURE

Rangers made it a hat-trick of successive cup wins with a narrow 1-0 win over Third Lanark, who had earlier seen off Falkirk at Tyncastle 3-1, while Rangers had coasted to a 3-0 win over Clyde.

1936-37 season saw Bo'ness sweep aside Border outfits with ease, with home wins over Coldstream 8-0, Gala Fairydean 5-0 and Peebles Rovers 3-0. Bo'ness eventually went down 2-1 to Duns away from home. This was enough to set up another Scottish Cup tie at Newtown Park, this time seeing the visit of Second Division Cowdenbeath. This took place in front of a rather disappointing attendance, around 1.000. Fewer than twenty attended from Fife, this was mainly down to the atrocious weather conditions and prior to the match it was down to a few volunteers who had the difficult job in clearing the snow from the pitch. Nevertheless this was achieved and although the surface was heavy and treacherous, it was deemed playable. It would be no exaggeration to say that Cowdenbeath won the match on the spin of a coin, as they had the good fortune to win the toss and the Fifers captain had no hesitation to play with the strong easterly wind, bringing with it a heavy snowfall. The game was over as a contest well before the half-time whistle, as a very poor Bo'ness defence put up very little resistance from the fast and furious Cowdenbeath forward line. They went in at the interval leading 5-0. Bo'ness looked a better team in the second half, but in all fairness Cowdenbeath had eased off considerably and seemed content to hold Bo'ness in check, and just to prove that point, they added sixth and final goal before the end.

THE BIGGER PICTURE

Aberdeen made their first Scottish Cup final appearance in front of a 146,433 crowd, a British record for a club match. Celtic, who had seen off Clyde, with Aberdeen beating Morton both by a 2-0 scoreline. Celtic won the final tie 2-1.

In Scottish Qualifying Cup, Bo'ness made their fourth final appearance and once again ended up beaten finalists. After defeating Duns, Murrayfield Amateurs, Penicuik Athletic and Vale of Leithen, they met Stranraer in the final at Somerset Park in Ayr. The Bo'ness team which lined up for their last Qualifying Cup final was as follows;

Welsh, Trotter, Durkin, Roughead, Quigg, Buchanan, Ritchie, P.Cowan, Henderson, D. Cowan and Miller

Over five hundred supporters travelled down to Ayrshire and witnessed an eight goal thriller. By the time the half-time whistle blew, Bo'ness found themselves 3-1 down, but the most amazing thing of all was the fact that the Stranraer keeper saved three penalty kicks. D. Cowan missed the first spot kick after only two minutes, which was then followed by misses from Henderson and Ritchie. Henderson however was the first-half scorer. Soon after the interval Stranraer added a fourth but the game was far from finished. With sixty-five minutes on the clock, it was Ritchie's turn to make amends of his spot kick miss by hammering home a full forty-five yard drive into the corner of the net, after a quick free kick had caught Stranraer unawares. Bo'ness, now beginning to believe in themselves and it was no surprise when Ritchie reduced Stranraer's lead to just one goal.

126

Moments later after an inviting pass from Miller, Ritchie squandered a great chance of a hat-trick and an equalising goal for the West Lothian side. It was all Bo'ness as they pressed forward for that fourth goal, and as the minutes ticked away, the Stranraer support was screaming out for the full time whistle. To their relief seconds from time, the match was wrapped up with a fifth and final goal for the Stair Park side, which once again left Bo'ness cursing their luck in a competition that has eluded them.

The Scottish Cup draw was once again kind to Bo'ness, when they were drawn at home against top league opponents Hamilton Academicals. The gulf between the clubs could not have been greater, as at that time Bo'ness' fixtures consisted of cup ties and friendlies, after the club had been refused entry to the East of Scotland League. Prior to the match the clubs directors signed up no fewer than five new recruits, in a bid to bolster up the squad.

The match itself went to plan and there was to be no cup shock for the Bo'ness support in the 2,591 attendance. The First Division clubs superior fitness proved all too much for the Bo'ness side as the Lanarkshire men strolled to victory with two goals either half. Although Bo'ness lost to a four goal margin, they were probably a little unlucky to see what would have been the opening goal, just after the fifteenth minute mark, judged to be offside, much to the despair of the home forwards.

THE BIGGER PICTURE

Two Second Division sides battled it out for a place in the final, eventually after three matches, all played at Tynecastle, East Fife made it through with a 2-1 victory over St Bernards, the other two games finishing 1-1. The other semi-final saw a seven goal thriller as Kilmarnock edged past Rangers with a 4-3 win. East Fife went into the history books as being the only lower league side to lift the Scottish Cup, defeating Kilmarnock 4-2 after a 1-1 draw, to this day are still the only team to achieve this feat.

Season 1938-39 was to see Bo'ness FC's last ever Scottish Qualifying/ Scottish Cup campaign, victories over Chirnside United and Selkirk before a narrow 3-2 defeat by Berwick Rangers was enough to earn a place in the first round draw of the Scottish Cup. As it turned out, it was fitting the club finished their long acquaintance in the competition bowing out with a home tie once again with the visit of Hamilton Academical.

The last team to take the field on Scottish Cup duty was as follows
Hunter, Patrick and R. Miller, Kennedy, Higgins and W. Miller, Peat, Innes and Hoy. Drumgoole and Holt

Watched on by a crowd of 3,000, it took Hamilton less than three minutes to open their account, Bo'ness nearly gifted the visitors with a second goal a minute later when an ill-timed pass back by R Miller struck the post with Hunter beaten. Play began to get scrappy with some wild tackles coming in from Bo'ness, King of Hamilton went down badly injured and had to retire after being sandwiched between Higgins and W. Miller. With Hamilton down to ten men, Bo'ness equalised on the half hour mark, a fine cross from Kennedy was headed into the net by Peat. Before half-time both clubs were down to ten men as Drumgoole was carried off with an ankle injury. After the interval Hamilton took control of the game and added a further three goals to run out deserved winners and bring an end to Bo'ness' cup campaign.

THE BIGGER PICTURE

A 1-0 win for Clyde over Hibernian at Tynecastle set up a final meeting with Motherwell who had disposed of Aberdeen 3-1 after a 1-1 draw.

The last pre war final saw Clyde make it third time lucky with an easy 4-0 victory over the Lanarkshire men.

With the Second World War disrupting the National competitions it was not until 1946-47 season that the Scottish Qualifying Cup returned. Bo'ness were drawn to play Coldstream away, but the Newtown Park Club scratched well before the tie was due to take place, Bo'ness FC had held a meeting and it was unanimously decided to abandon all proposals to reconstitute a senior team. Instead it was decided to go ahead with the formation of a Junior club in the name of Bo'ness United.

THE BIGGER PICTURE

Aberdeen celebrated the cup's return with a 2-1 win over Hibernian. The next three finals belonged to Rangers with victories over Morton, 1-0 (1-1), Clyde 4-1, and East Fife, 3-0. The replayed final against Morton set a record attendance for a British midweek gate of 133,570. 1949 saw Second Division Dundee United shock Celtic with a 4-3 first round win at Tannadice.

1951 saw Celtic collect the trophy for the sixteenth time defeating Motherwell 1-0, the Fir Park side only had to wait a season to finally get their hands on the trophy defeating Dundee 4-0.

Aberdeen contested the next two finals but lost them both against the Old Firm, first they lost to Rangers 1-0 after a 1-1 draw, then to Celtic, going down 2-1.

1955 saw Clyde's name go on the trophy defeating Celtic 1-0 after a 1-1 draw, Celtic were again runners up the following season with Heart of Midlothian taking the cup back to Tynecastle with a 3-1 victory, exactly fifty years since their last success.

Underdogs Falkirk lifted the cup for a second time with a 2-1 win over Kilmarnock after extra time, after the first match ended in a 1-1 draw.

1958 saw Clyde win 1-0 against Hibernian in what was a scrappy encounter.

The following season St Mirren got the better of Aberdeen in a 3-1 win, Saints had earlier scored four without reply against Celtic in the semi finals. In the first round that year Highland League side Fraserburgh defeated high flying First Division side Dundee 1-0 at home.

1960 saw Rangers lift the Cup defeating Kilmarnock 2-0.

Dunfermline Athletic won the trophy for the first time in 1961 defeating Celtic 2-0 after a 0-0 draw; by 1965 both teams were back at Hampden but this time round Celtic defeated the Fifers 3-2 with Jock Stein managing the cup winners on both occasions.

In between these matches saw another hat-trick of successes for Rangers, 1962 saw a 2-0 win over St Mirren, the following year it took a replay to see off Celtic with a 3-0 win after a 1-1 draw, the two matches watched by an incredible 250,000 spectators. The 1964 final saw a 3-1 win over Dundee.

In 1966 the Old Firm met again with Rangers lifting the trophy for the 19th time with a 1-0 win after the first match ended goal-less.
The following year Celtic equalled Rangers total of Scottish cup wins with a 2-0 win over Aberdeen, but the main talking point and arguably the biggest upsets in the tournament's history was Rangers 1-0 defeat to Second Division Berwick Rangers.

Dunfermline Athletic won the trophy again in 1968 with a 3-1 win over Heart of Midlothian. With both Celtic and Rangers playing for their twentieth trophy win it was the former that came out on top with a 4-0 win. Aberdeen collected the cup for the second time with a 3-1 win over Celtic. The following year saw another Old Firm final, Celtic coming out on top with a 2-1 win after a 1-1 draw, both matches attracting 100,000 plus gates. 1972 saw Celtic retain the Cup, as mentioned previously they equalled the record score in a cup final defeating Hibernian 6-1.

In 1973, Rangers came out on top with a 3-2 victory over their Old Firm rivals. That year in the Scottish Qualifying Cup Edinburgh works team Ferranti Thistle made their first appearance in the competition. By reaching the semi final stages they qualified for the Scottish Cup, before losing out to Elgin City in the second round. It was in later years that this club was to bring senior football back to West Lothian.

1974 saw Dundee United make their first ever final appearance, but there was to be no shocks as Celtic won comfortably 3-0. The following year Celtic held on to the trophy with a 3-1 win over Airdrieonians.

The Glasgow giants continued to dominate the seventies with the trophy heading back to Ibrox in 1976 after Rangers defeated Heart of Midlothian by a 3-1 scoreline. Celtic and Rangers clashed again in the1977 Cup Final with the Parkhead side taking the honours with a 1-0 win.

The next two years belonged to Rangers, first was a 2-1 win over Aberdeen followed by a 3-2 victory over Hibernian after two 0-0 draws. Celtic won the first cup in the eighties, winning by a single goal in extra time over Rangers; this final however will always be remembered for the scenes after the final whistle as rival fans fought out a pitched battle on the Hampden turf.

1981 once again saw the trophy heading back over to the other side of the city as Rangers saw off Dundee United 4-1 after a 0-0 draw.

The Old Firm's stranglehold finally came to an end and once again it was to be Aberdeen's name that was to grace the trophy. This time round all the same was to be no "flash in the pan", as the Dons went on to win a hat-trick of Cups, the first team to achieve such a feat out with the Old Firm since Queens Park and Vale of Leven did so in the opening six years of the competition. All three finals went to extra time, the first two against Rangers ended 4-1 and 1-0 with the third resulting in a 2-1 win over Celtic.

Celtic beat Dundee United 2-1 in the 1985 final, but it was to be Aberdeen who were to lift the Cup the following season 3-0, seeing of a dejected Heart of Midlothian side who had lost the League Championship on the final day of the season the previous week.

A cup win for Dundee United continued to elude them as St Mirren scored an extra time winner to take the trophy back to Paisley for the first time since 1959.

The following year Dundee United were again runners-up with Celtic once more inflicting the damage with a 2-1 scoreline.

1989 saw Celtic retain the trophy with another 1-0 win over rivals Rangers, this time though without the pitch battle!

1990 saw the first Cup Final to be decided in penalty kicks, after ninety minutes plus the thirty minutes extra time both Aberdeen and Celtic had failed to hit the net, Aberdeen eventually lifted the Cup with an incredible 9-8 penalty kick showdown.

1991 saw another incredible match with Motherwell and Dundee United playing out a seven goal thriller where Dundee United failed to get their hands on the trophy yet again.

The 1992 final saw Rangers defeat Airdrieonians 2-1; they repeated the scoreline the following season with a victory over Aberdeen.

1994 eventually saw the Cup heading to Tannadice, as Dundee United saw off Rangers with a 1-0 win, it was the clubs seventh final in twenty years.
Airdrieonians made yet another final in 1995, this time losing out to the other half of the Old Firm 1-0.

West Lothian again had a senior football team competing for the National Trophy in the shape of Livingston FC; this was not a new team however, but a struggling Edinburgh outfit who were always in the shadows of the city's big two Heart of Midlothian and Hibernian. This club was admitted into the Scottish League in season 1974-75, when the league eventually evened up after the demise of Third Lanark in 1967, and also with the reconstruction to the Scottish League being just round the corner an extra team was needed. As previously mentioned it was to be works team Ferranti Thistle who won the place. Due to the Scottish League's strict rules in advertising/sponsorship at that time, the club had to change their name with Meadowbank Thistle being the preferred option.

Looking at Meadowbank's Scottish Cup record it was pretty poor, with the club never managing to get past the fourth round stages. It was when chairman Bill Hunter announced that the club were struggling financially, that Livingston Development Corporation decided to step in and relocate the club and build a brand new stadium in Livingston. The small band of loyal supporters were up in arms, but the change over went ahead against their wishes with yet another new name "to boot", Livingston Football Club.

The Club's first game in the "Scottish" under their new name resulted in a 3-0 win over Stranraer, the Stair Park club had been unbeaten at home up until this game and being a league above Livingston had been tipped to continue their fine form. Livingston had keeper Robert Douglas (later to become a Scotland Internationalist) to thank however for a series of early saves, he also saved a second half penalty with Livingston leading 2-0 at the time would have certainly brought the home side back into the game. As it worked out, the visitors scored a third to tie up the match. Goals coming from Mark Duthie along with a Graham Harvey double. The second round saw the Club on their travels once again, this time to play Caledonian Thistle, at Telford Street Park. In what was described as a Jekyll and Hyde performance, Caley found themselves two up after twenty-five minutes. After the interval however, Livingston managed to pull back to 2-2, goals once again courtesy of Mark Duthie and Graham Harvey, but disappointingly lost a third goal moments later, this proved to be the decisive goal and sent the Almondvale side out the cup.

Livingston's "first" Scottish Cup Programme © Mr.David Stoker

THE BIGGER PICTURE

Rangers strolled to victory, lifting the Cup with a superb 5-1 victory over Heart of Midlothian, the Glasgow side were in fine goal scoring form, in the third round they hammered ten past Highland League side Keith at Pittodrie.

After receiving a bye in the first round of the 1996-97 campaign, Livingston were drawn away to Brechin City. The original tie postponed due to poor weather finally went ahead on the Monday night. Former player Stuart Sorbie opened the scoring for City after fourteen minutes, Livingston did come close on a few occasions but it was to be Sorbie again who found the net five minutes before the interval. Livingston mounted tremendous pressure in the second half, even though substitute Lee Bailey pulled one back, they never found an equaliser that could have forced a replay back at Almondvale.

THE BIGGER PICTURE

Kilmarnock and Falkirk took part in the 1997 final. Falkirk defeating Celtic 1-0 after a replay at the semi-final stages. The "Bairns" must have fancied their chances, but as usual in football it doesn't always turn out that way, as on this occasion Kilmarnock went on to lift the trophy with a Paul Wright goal after twenty minutes, watched on by a crowd of just under 49,000.

1997-98 season and Livingston finally got a home tie in the competition, after receiving a first round bye, where they entertained Berwick Rangers at Almondvale. With the first match being postponed, the tie went ahead on the Wednesday in front of just over 950 spectators on a bitterly cold night. Livingston created many first half chances but the game remained goal-less at the interval. Graham Harvey opened the scoring on the hour mark for "Livi", however Berwick were on level terms within five minutes when a long range effort totally deceived keeper Ian McCaldon and ended up in the back of the net. Within a minute the home side were back in front when Grant McMartin bulleted home a diving header which proved to be the decisive goal.

The third round saw the visit of Albion Rovers to Almondvale, Livingston started brightly with Gordon Forrest and Mark Duthie scoring in the opening twenty minutes. The home side had several opportunities to put the tie beyond doubt, but they seemed to take their foot off the pedal, which allowed Rovers to come back into the game. On the half hour mark McCaldon fumbled a cross ball to allow the visitors back into the match. Ten minutes later Graham Davidson was ordered off for a last man foul, which resulted in Rovers equalising from the resulting free kick and rounding of an entertaining first half. The second half was a complete contrast, when a dour ten man Livingston took the lead again this time through Graham Harvey ten minutes into the second half. As the minutes ticked away it seemed as if ten man Livi had weathered the storm, but with only seconds remaining Albion struck to force a replay.

With electrical problems at Cliftonhill the match was switched to East Stirlingshire's Firs Park. After two hours of football, both teams failed to find the net resulting in a penalty shootout that went on to sudden death and when Livingston's McMartin had his attempt punched to safety it was all over. With rumours of financial problems surfacing at Almondvale stadium it was most disappointing to lose out to Third Division Albion Rovers when a fourth round tie against Heart of Midlothian at Tynecastle lay in wait for the winners.

THE BIGGER PICTURE

Heart of Midlothian gained revenge over Rangers from the 5-1 defeat a couple of years earlier with a 2-1 win, a late McCoist goal gave the Hearts support a nervy last ten minutes before they watched their side collect the National trophy for the first time since 1956.

Livingston made heavy weather of their first round tie at Dumbarton's Boghead ground, when just before half-time Jim Sherry was given his marching orders for protesting a tackle. They did however take the lead in the fifty-eighth minute when John Millar scored from close range with a diving header. It was then down to keeper Neil Alexander in the Livi goal who produced a string of top class saves, with five minutes remaining however, he was finally beaten, but ten man Livingston held out for a replay.

The first half of the replayed tie was totally dominated by Livingston but all they had to show for their efforts was a one goal lead, and even at that, was an own goal. Dumbarton had their best spell at the beginning of the second half, but after seventy minutes Livingston added a second through Derek Fleming, and just on the final whistle David Bingham wrapped up the scoring with a delightful twenty-five yard lob into the far corner of the net.

The second round once again saw Livingston travel to Inverness, but this time they came back with a victory. A ninth minute penalty was converted by Bingham, but just on the stroke of half-time the sides were level, as Alexander parried out a shot it came off McManus' head and into the net for an own goal. The winning goal was scored just after the hour when Mark McCormack beat the offside trap to slam home the winner.

The third round brought an interesting tie as Livingston travelled to Pittodrie to take on Premier League side Aberdeen. An estimated 1800 fans travelled up from West Lothian to cheer the side on, and that they certainly did as head coach Ray Stewart quoted "it was like playing with an extra man". The match itself was decided in the sixty-first minute when Livingston's veteran striker John Robertson latched on to an Ian Little pass thirty-five yards out to calmly tuck the ball past the advancing keeper. Aberdeen created a few chances but found Alexander in top form, as Aberdeen pushed players forward both McPhee and Forrest had chances to kill of the game but in the end Robertson's strike was enough to take Livingston into the next round. Their reward was for the Pittodrie triumph was a match against another Premier League outfit, where St Johnstone would be visitors for the fourth round tie. A record gate of 5,788 (just short of the 6,015 capacity at the time) watched in hope to see the club progress to the next round, as it turned out a well organised Saints side were always in control and eased through to the next round with a 3-1 victory. St Johnstone striker Roddy Grant a Livingston local would not have been the most popular person in the town that night as he carried away the man of the match award, for the record it was John Robertson who popped up to score Livingston's late consolation goal.

THE BIGGER PICTURE

Both Celtic and Rangers strolled into the final with semi-final wins over Dundee United 2-0 and St Johnstone 4-0 respectively. A Rod Wallace goal just after half-time was all that separated the sides and see the trophy head back to Ibrox.

Livingston started their 1999-2000 cup campaign in fine style as they rattled seven goals past hapless Queen of the South at Palmerston Park (a record competitive win for Meadowbank/Livingston). Livingston went in at half-time with a single goal lead thanks to Ray McKinnon, but Queen's having a man sent off after twenty three minutes put Livingston on easy street. After the break Livingston seized control with a quick fire hat-trick from Marino Keith (51, 58, and 63 minutes) which finished the tie but not before an Alan Kerr own goal made it five, McPhee grabbed a sixth, then right at the end McKinnon added his second and Livingston's seventh with a spectacular long range effort.

Hopes were dashed of another cup run when Second Division Partick Thistle sent Livingston crashing out of the competition. A lacklustre Livingston side gave one of their most disappointing performances of the season; it seemed different early on as Bingham volleyed home after only eight minutes, a series of fine saves from the Thistle keeper kept his side in the tie. Livingston seemed happy to cruise into the next round but were in for a shock just before half-time when the home side grabbed an equaliser. Worse was to follow for Livingston when Marc Millar received two yellow cards in a space of eight minutes to leave the West Lothian men an uphill struggle for the closing minutes of the game. As it turned out Thistle took full advantage and went on to grab a second and earn a shock victory.

THE BIGGER PICTURE

Rangers were in fine goalscoring form hitting seven goals past Ayr United in the semi-final stages, Aberdeen booked the other slot coming back from a goal down to see off Hibernian with a 2-1 victory. The final will be remembered for the injury of Aberdeen keeper Jim Leighton after only three minutes of the game played, as he was unable to continue and Aberdeen having no substitute keeper on the bench; Robbie Winters had to take his place in goal. As it turned out Rangers strolled to a 4-0 victory, three of the goals coming from a four minute spell at the start of the second half.

Livingston were on the road, with an away trip to Methil, once again they made things difficult for themselves being reduced to ten men after a late Stevie Tosh tackle, this was after East Fife had taken the lead. Livingston however proved too strong for the Fifers with Bingham equalising before a great double from Barry Wilson secured the tie, Gerry Britton rounded off the scoring for the visitors with a 4-1 victory.

Premier league Aberdeen visited Almondvale for the fourth round tie and somehow managed to leave with their cup dreams still intact with a goalless draw. Livingston outshone their opponents in all departments but had they been a little more clinical up front there would have been no need to travel up to Pittodrie in midweek.

With the draw for the fifth round being made Livingston knew that winning the replay could send them into the semi-finals as all that was between them was Third Division Peterhead, with this added incentive Livingston came out on top with a 1-0 victory. The match looked as if it was going into extra time till Scott Crabbe stepped off the bench to head home the winner with only seven minutes remaining.

Peterhead certainly showed that they were not just here to make up the numbers as they came out with all guns blazing, and deservedly took the lead after only seven minutes. There was no stopping Livingston however, the man who made the difference was defender John Anderson, when he grabbed a double and set up Bingham to grab the third and final goal to send Livingston into the semi-finals at Hampden Park, the first for a West Lothian side since Broxburn Shamrock did likewise back in 1893.

The Club laid on fifty free buses as around 4,500 supporters left West Lothian hoping to see their side make history by reaching the Scottish Cup final and help swell the gates to over 24,500. The Livingston side that day was as follows:-

McCaldon, Brinquin, Fleming, Anderson, Andrews, Deas, Tosh, McCulloch, Wilson, Burns, Bingham, Subs, Jackson, Hagan, Britton, (Hart and McEwan not used)

Ian McCaldon only played following cortisone injections, regular keeper Alexander had broke his hand a few weeks previously. There had been suggestions of signing Celtic's squad keeper Dimitri Kharine on an emergency loan. The game was a bit of a non event with Livingston going a goal down after only eighty seconds. With Hibernian in command, Livingston had keeper McCaldon to thank as he produced a string of fine saves to keep Livingston's dreams alive. However with only twenty minutes remaining, the keeper was at fault when he and Marvin Andrews tangled on the edge of the box, this allowed Hibs to wrap up the tie with a second goal, the now confident Edinburgh side added a third ten minutes later to complete the scoring. Livingston had the consolation of winning the First Division and promotion to the SPL few weeks later at Inverness.

THE BIGGER PICTURE

Celtic defeated Dundee United 3-1 to book their place in the final against Hibernian. Celtic went on to lift the trophy; McNamara opened the scoring for Celtic just before half time, Larsson added a second just after the interval then rounded off the scoring from the penalty spot with ten minutes remaining.

A third round tie against lower league Albion Rovers caused very few problems to newly promoted Premier League Livingston, probably the biggest obstacle were the floodlights at Cliftonhill which failed to shine on a heavy pitch. After the interval and a forty minute delay with the game tied at 0-0 the game was eventually abandoned, this was a lucky escape for a poor Livingston team that night. The rearranged match went ahead in front of 2,234 spectators, (mainly down to free admission) at Airdrieonians New Broomfield Park, where the West Lothian side ran out easy 4-1 winners, goals coming from Barry Wilson, David Bingham (2) and David Fernandez.

The fourth round saw Livingston head up north to take on Aberdeen, a third time since the club's move to Livingston. Aberdeen were certainly fired up for this match after their two previous defeats to the New Town club. A couple of quick fire goals from Robbie Winters and Jamie McAllister, (both future Livingston signings) settled the Dons as they dominated the early stages of the match, although both teams produced one or two chances there was to be no further scoring, all in all Aberdeen merited their victory overall.

THE BIGGER PICTURE

Celtic and Rangers saw off their First Division opponents Ayr United and Partick Thistle with 3-0 victories to set up another Old Firm final. It was to be Rangers who went on to lift the trophy thanks to a last minute Peter Lovenkrands goal which gave the Ibrox club a 3-2 victory.

Livingston failed at the first hurdle of the 2002-03 Cup campaign, after receiving a home tie they failed to take advantage of a struggling Dunfermline side. A Gary Bollan goal midway through the first half was all they had to show from the numerous chances they created. This was to come back and haunt the Almondvale side as the Pars equalised in the sixty third minute. Till the end of the match both teams went all out for the winner but there was to be no further scoring. The replay at East End Park shown live on TV on what was a bitterly cold night. Youngster Dave McEwan replaced Javier Sanchez Broto in goal after his transfer to Celtic, he had a terrible game, the Sun headline the following day summed it up "Dave Threwin". End of the day a Craig Brewster double gave Dunfermline a deserved win and sent Livingston spinning out the Cup.

THE BIGGER PICTURE

In the semi-final ties Rangers saw off Motherwell 4-3 while Dundee scored the only goal of the game against Inverness Caledonian Thistle.
A single Amoruso strike was all that separated the sides in the final, watched on by 47,136 spectators.

After the previous season's early exit, Livingston certainly made amends by reaching the semi-final stages once again. The run started with a 1-0 victory over Montrose courtesy of a magnificent long range effort from old favourite David Fernandez on loan from Celtic.
It was down memory lane for the fourth round tie, as Livingston visited their old ground City Park, when in their early days they played their home matches as Ferranti Thistle before moving to Meadowbank Stadium.

Opponent's non league Spartans had produced a few cup shocks in recent seasons and were well up for a crack against Premier League opposition. With the City Park dressing rooms not to Livingston's standards it was decided to use Hibernian's Easter Road facilities where they stripped for the game and arrived by coach and did likewise immediately after the final whistle. An all ticket crowd of 3,123 watched on, as the non-league outfit gave as good as they got in the opening forty- five minutes. Into the second half however and Livingston stepped up a gear with three quick goals, Derek Lilley scoring in the fifty-third and sixty-first minute. With Fernandez goal in-between, Lilley completed his hat-trick after seventy minutes to complete the scoring. The following Wednesday after this tie Livingston found themselves in administration.

The quarter-final tie saw Livingston paired with Aberdeen at Pittodrie, an all so familiar tie. After a five goal thriller earlier on in the season between the two sides in a League Cup match, it was clear to see there would be no repeat on the goals front as both teams started off nervously, with very little goalmouth action. Livi's ex Don Jamie McAllister had the first real crack at goal, forcing the home keeper into a superb save after unleashing a thirty-five yard drive, before the first forty-five ended Livi keeper Roddy McKenzie came to the rescue with a fine double save.

Six minutes into the second half and Livingston took the lead, through an own goal from Dons skipper Anderson. The West Lothian's side lead was short lived however as Aberdeen were back on level terms with a deflected shot. Livingston had several chances to win the match, Derek Lilley in particular being unlucky on a few occasions, but by the end of the day the game remained level and a replay required.

Livingston in action against Aberdeen © Mr. David Stoker

Four days after Livingston's League Cup triumph over Hibernian at Hampden Park, Aberdeen travelled down to the County where they were tipped to see off an exhausted Livi side. Aberdeen had all the early possession but it was to be the home side who were to open the scoring. David Fernandez put the Don's keeper under pressure at the edge of the box, forcing him to make a poor clearance. The ball fell to Burton O'Brien thirty-five yards out,who in turn unleashed a dipping left foot shot into the empty net, this was to prove the only goal of the game and set up Livingston for another Hampden day out.

For the second time in recent seasons Livingston made the semi-final stages of the competition, this time round they were drawn against Celtic, the Glasgow giants proved too much for the Livingston outfit who on the day had to do without the services of David Fenandez as he was on loan from Celtic at that time. The game watched on by 26,152, in what was a rather wet day.The game however started brightly for Livi who carved open the first chance of the match as Derek Lilley forced a great save from Celtic keeper Marshall. As the game progressed Celtic took command and it was no surprise when Sutton opened the scoring in the thirty-seventh minute, five minutes after the interval Larsson took advantage of a defensive mix-up between McNamee and Dorado to double their lead. With ten minutes remaining Celtic wrapped up the tie when Sutton scored his second, with just over ten minutes remaining McMenamin scored a consolation for Livingston to end the scoring.

THE BIGGER PICTURE

Inverness Caledonian Thistle competed in their second successive semi-final, this time losing out to Dunfermline Athletic 3-2 after a 1-1 draw. With Celtic's 3-1 win over Livingston, the scoreline was repeated in the final, Larsson hitting a double in what was to be his last competitive game for the club.

In the 2004-05 Scottish Cup, Livingston kicked off their campaign against Morton in the most unbearable conditions as gale force winds and heavy rain lashed down on the Almondvale pitch. In a game that should never have gone ahead, the visitors with the wind at their backs had the bulk of possession in the first half, it was however, Livingston who took the lead after thirty-six minutes when Rubio half volleyed into the net. Morton responded immediately to level the scores. It was not until around the seventy minute mark that Livingston restored their lead when substitute Robert Snodgrass rifled home from close range in what was to prove to be the winner.

Livingston were second out of the hat for the second round draw resulting in a trip over to Recreation Park to take on Alloa Athletic. Returning from injury Colin McMenamin came off the bench in the second period to grab the winner with only seconds remaining to record a rather fortunate victory for the struggling Almondvale side.

Another away tie this time saw Richard Gough's Livingston travel through to the capital to take on Heart of Midlothian. The "Lions" were caught napping as they found themselves a goal down in the first minute, but worse was to follow when a second goal was conceded after only ten minutes. Holding out till halftime Livingston rearranged their team by bringing on all substitutes, which seemed to steady the team and they managed to claw themselves back into the game, after Craig Easton pulled a goal back on the hour mark. Livingston continued to put pressure on the home defence but it was Hearts who were to hold on for a semi-final place.

THE BIGGER PICTURE

With Dundee United beating Hibernian 2-1, and Celtic seeing off Hearts by the same scoreline, there was to be no capital final. A Thompson strike after eleven minutes was enough to see Celtic win the 120th Scottish Cup.

Alloa Athletic gained some revenge from last season and knocked Livingston out of the cup at the first hurdle. The first game ended in a 1-1 draw at Alloa, thanks to a injury time Richard Brittain equaliser. A disappointing Livingston side failed to make home advantage. A Paul Dalglish, son of Kenny scored from the spot to put Livi ahead, but Second Division Alloa battled back to record a 2-1 victory their winner coming nine minutes from time. Livingston were relegated that season with a record low points tally, Paul Lambert was manager during this period.

THE BIGGER PICTURE

Gretna continued to shock as they made their way to the final with an emphatic 3-0 win over Dundee. Hearts went one better against city rivals Hibernian with a 4-0 victory. Second division Gretna fought all the way taking Hearts into extra time after a 1-1 draw and then to penalty kicks. Hearts however kept their cool to win 4-2 from the spot. Lowly First Division Clyde knocked out Celtic 2-1 at Broadwood to produce the shock of the year.

Two goals from Graham Dorrans set up an easy cup win over Hamilton Academicals, with his first goal giving Livingston the interval lead. Accies managed to get back on level terms, however Steven Tweed restored the lead for the Lion's after the sixty-fifth minute. Eight minutes later Hamill added a third and Dorrans grabbed his second with ten minutes still remaining. Accies scored a consolation in the final few minutes to round off the scoring.

Celtic visited Almondvale for the fourth round clash, where an attendance of 7,281 along with the many who watched live coverage on Sky. The visitors were given a fright, after just eighteen minutes Dave Mackay headed home the opener. Celtic proved too much for the First Division side however, equalising after thirty minutes. They then went on to snatch the lead just on the half-time whistle. Celtic killed off the tie on the hour mark with a quick double, to end any hope of a Livi' fight back.

THE BIGGER PICTURE

Semi-finals saw Celtic defeat St Johnstone 2-1 with Dunfermline earning their place with a 1-0 replay win after a goalless first match with Hibernian.

Despite being relegated Dunfermline had also knocked out Rangers and Heart of Midlothian on route to the final, Celtic proved one hurdle to much for the Fife side, but it took a late goal to secure the win.

Season 2007-08 saw a change in format for the Scottish Cup, for the first time since the mid fifties there was to be no Qualifying Cup Competitions, with all the usual candidates entered into the first round draw, not only that but for the first time ever we saw Junior sides enter the National Trophy. Junior Super League champions as well as Junior Cup winners had the chance to pit their wits against the country's "elite".

As it turned out Linlithgow Rose defeated Kelty Hearts in the Junior Cup Final and they also ran out league champions just for good measure to earn themselves a shot of glory and enter the club into the record books. Linlithgow's first ever match in the "big" Scottish Cup saw them travel south to take on non league seniors Newton Stewart from the South of Scotland league. The Rose side that made history that day was as follows

Pinkowski, Tyrell, Donnelly, Denham, McDermott, McAthur, Hogg, Bradley, McSween, Carrigan, and Herd.
Substitutes, McGlynn, Courts, Donaldson, Feeney, Burnet,

It wasn't until the thirtieth minute that Linlithgow eventually opened their account from the penalty spot, Carrigan the scorer, just on half time. Herd doubled the lead, within a minute of the restart McArthur added a third, McSween made certain of victory by scoring Linlithgow's fourth after seventy minutes. In the final five minutes Carrigan and Herd doubled their tallies to get the West Lothian side off to the best possible start.

The second round saw Linlithgow drawn at home against "top dogs" from the east Spartans, a team desperately keen to step up to the Scottish League and certainly a team who have done themselves no harm in recent seasons by shocking a few league sides in the Cup. A crowd of 1,519, which was just less than double the size (819) that watched West Lothian neighbours Livingston at Almondvale on the same day, proved just how big an outfit Linlithgow are on the Junior circuit.

Played in traditional cup-tie fashion, both teams were clearly fired up for the challenge.

Spartans had the best chance after fifteen minutes, midfielder King somehow managed to escape punishment for a blatant elbow on Rose's Scottish Junior International Keith Hogg. As the ball broke forward, Spartans raced up field, Rose keeper McGlynn however did well to block. As the ball broke lose and the keeper still grounded, the visitors ruined a simple chance to open the scoring ,with the goal gaping, the ball was screwed into the side netting. Spartans were left to rue that chance, as just over five minutes later Linlithgow opened the scoring. After fine work from McArthur down the left wing, as the ball came over Bradley was on hand to side foot the ball into the net for the only goal of the first half. With Prestonfield now buzzing with excitement the visitors did manage to quieten them for a short spell, as they equalised from the spot in the fifty-fourth minute. Linlithgow were quick to reply however and just over five minutes later regained the lead through McArthur. With twelve minutes remaining the tie was clinched when Tyrell headed home a third and just to make sure Hogg curled home a fourth a minute later to round off a magnificent performance.

The third round saw Linlithgow drawn at home against Dalbeattie Star. Again a large crowd of 1,500 gathered at Prestonfield and witnessed another Linlithgow victory, this time however was a tighter affair,with only one goal in the match coming after two minutes, McArthur the scorer.

Livingston, on the other hand, had no such problems with a home victory over Alloa Athletic, Julius Ralikonus opened the scoring after thirty-three minutes. Then in a nine minute spell around the hour mark a Mackay double and a Keaghan Jacobs effort on his first team debut rounded of a 4-0 win.

The fourth round eventually brought around league opposition for Linlithgow in the shape of first division Queen of the South. With a large following Rose set off for Dumfries, but there was to be no cup shock as Queens sweep aside their Junior opponents, leading 3-0 at half-time. A McArthur own goal in the seventy-second minute ended the scoring, although far from disgraced, the eventual Scottish Cup runners-up proved too difficult a hurdle for the Junior outfit.

Over at Almondvale Livingston had a relaxing afternoon as they strolled to victory, a Craig goal after only four minutes followed up by a McMenamin goal just after the half hour mark was enough to see past Cowdenbeath and into the next round.

Livingston and Partick Thistle failed to score at Almondvale, and the replay at Firhill also finished level. Livingston could feel rather unfortunate not reaching the quarter-finals after Dorrans had given them the lead just before half time.It took a late equaliser to send the game into extra time. With no further scoring it was to be Thistle that held their nerve winning 5-4 in the penalty shoot out, Dave Mackay the regular penalty taker put his kick over the bar and end what would have seen a lucrative trip to Ibrox.

THE BIGGER PICTURE

Rangers struggled into the final eventually seeing off St Johnstone in a penalty shoot out. Shock troops Queen of the South reached their first ever final with an amazing 4-3 win over Aberdeen, all goals coming within the first hour.

Queens made Rangers fight all the way, trailing 2-0 at half time the Palmerston Park side scored a quick double just after the break to draw level. In the end however it was to be Rangers who were to score that decisive third goal and take the trophy back to Ibrox.

Another new name appeared in the competition as Bathgate Thistle lifted the Scottish Junior Cup. Willie Hill's men defeating Cumnock 2-1 in the final thus gaining entry to the National trophy. Sadly Bathgate didn't get a run like Linlithgow the previous season, and were rather unfortunate to be drawn away from home against fellow league side Lochee United who had been crowned East Super League champions. Nevertheless the following side lined up for the club's first crack in the competition,

Carlin, Fallon, Neill, Love, Menmuir, Nicolson, Easton, McPhee, Harvey, McGrillen, and McColligan, Substitutes, Blaney, McFadyen, Wilson and Longmuir.

With a horrendous injury list, Bathgate were without many key players, with many of the injured forced to make the starting line up. With all their disadvantages Bathgate still managed to go in at the interval a goal up, thanks to a Paul Harvey penalty. In the second half however, Lochee seemed to step up a gear, but poor finishing from the homesters kept Bathgate in with a chance. This was was all to change as Lochee drew level in the seventieth minute through a debatable penalty. A bizarre second goal ten minutes later gave Lochee the lead, a free kick was touched on to the cross bar by keeper Carlin, only to bounce down and hit him on the back and roll into the net. Two minutes later the match was finished, the Bathgate defence failed to clear its lines and lost a third and final goal.

Courtesy of Graeme McGinty

Livingston completed a miserable year in the competition by going down first time of asking to Third Division East Stirlingshire at Ochilview. It was at this time of the ill fated Italian regime and manager Roberto Landi. Shire shocked Livingston with an opening goal after only nine minutes. A spectacular strike from Fox a fully thirty five yards out levelled the scores before half time. Shire scored a second and final goal ten minutes after the restart to seal a memorable victory for the lower league side.

THE BIGGER PICTURE

Rangers progressed to the final with a comfortable 3-0 win over St Mirren, while Falkirk were deserving winners over rivals Dunfermline Athletic with a 2-0 win.
A Novo goal a minute after the restart was enough to see Rangers retain the trophy.

With no West Lothian Junior sides winning any major competitions it was left to Livingston to fly the flag for the County. If it had not been for a last minute deal the financially stricken Almondvale club could easily have folded and joined the list of all the other senior sides in the district from years gone by. In the end a deal was struck, the club survived, but suffered a real blow by being demoted to the third division. Livingston opened up their 2009-10 Scottish Cup account which saw them make the visit to Hampden Park to take on Queens Park. There was to be no problems for Livi as they eased themselves into the third round. Robbie Winters set up De Vita who volleyed home for the opening goal after thirty-two minutes. Fox doubled the lead just after the hour, even though Queens Park pulled a goal back with twelve minutes remaining, Livingston restored their two goal advantage when Raffaele De Vita was on hand to knock home a Jacobs cross that had been dummied by Winters to end the scoring.

Livingston's third round tie with Clyde created a bit of history as the tie consisted of two abandonments, one postponement, and a stalemate before eventually being decided. Fog descending on Broadwood Stadium resulted in both matches being abandoned, with Livingston leading on both occasions (1-0, 2-1). Sandwiched in between was the postponement due to a frozen pitch then,to cap it all the sides could not be separated when the match was eventually played. Livingston's Moyes was sent packing just before half time after receiving his second booking.

Livingston however took the lead just after the interval, Joe Hamill with a spectacular back heeled effort (goal ended up in the Showboat slot on Sky's Soccer AM Show). Midway through the second half Clyde found the net to force a replay, though De Vita was rather unfortunate not to have won the tie for Livingston as he struck the post in the final minute. The replay at Almondvale saw Livingston coast into the next round with an astounding victory. An early Jacobs's goal was quickly cancelled out and there was to be no further scoring in the first forty-five. This was all to change however, as Livingston went goal crazy after the interval. An astonishing three goals in as many minutes set the pace, Fox scoring after 49 minutes followed by Winters in 50 minutes, then Andy Halliday in 51minutes which finished the tie as a contest. A further goal each from the trio capped a great night for Livingston, and an emphatic final score of 7-1, which turned out a record home win for Livingston.

With one of the worst winters in many years Livingston's next tie against Dundee took three attempts before finally getting the go ahead to play. It was certainly worth the wait, as the fans who turned up in a bitterly cold night were entertained to a typically old fashioned end to end cup tie. Both teams had chances to win several games, but as it turned out, a strike from Dundee's Harkins was all that separated the sides. Livingston's best chance fell to Liam Fox shortly after the only goal was scored, Winters running in on goal was brought down in the box, but Fox's poor spot kick was easily parried away by the Dundee keeper. Even though Livi matched the First Division high flyers in every department, it was not to be their night. To rub salt into the wounds former Livingston favourite Leigh Griffiths knowledge of the Almondvale side helped his side stay in front as he mentioned after the game that he had signalled to the Dundee keeper which side the spot kick would probably go.

THE BIGGER PICTURE

First Division side Ross County strolled into the Scottish Cup final for the first time in their history with an easy 2-0 win over Celtic. Raith Rovers failed to make it an all first division clash going down 2-0 to Dundee United. There was to be no shock in the final, as United went on to lift the trophy with a 3-0 victory, all goals coming in the second half.

Season 2010-11 produced the highest amount of entrants since the early 1930's. It was all down to Bo'ness United and Linlithgow Rose's success in Junior football. United won the League title while Rose lifted the Scottish Junior Cup, thus enabling the pair to join Livingston in the competition. Linlithgow were rather unfortunate to be drawn away to Junior counterparts Beith Juniors ,winners of the West Super League. Rose started off brightly considering their horrendous injury list, and dominated much of the first half-hour, kicking down hill on Beith's sloping pitch. Rose however, failed to capitalise as chance after chance went a-begging, with twenty-eight minutes on the clock the West Lothian side fell behind as the home side grabbed the opener against the run of play. Rose keeper Pinkowski came out to collect a cross ball but missed completely to leave a Beith forward the simple task to nod home at the far post. Beith took confidence from this and finished the stronger side as the half-time whistle blew. Linlithgow continued to struggle and were fortunate to still be in the game as the home side created a good few chances. Rose made a couple of substitutions bringing on King and MacLennan and for a while enjoyed more possession, which produced several half chances but failing to find an equaliser.

With ten minutes remaining Beith wrapped up the tie with a second goal, the home side saw out the last ten minutes comfortably, and deservedly went into the second round draw. Bo'ness took a trip down to the Borders to take on East of Scotland league side Selkirk, accompanied by a large travelling support. The BU's didn't let them down, as they ran out easy winners with an easy 6-1 victory over their hapless hosts.

Lining up for their first ever Scottish Cup tie the Bo'ness team was as follows

McGurk, Snowdon, Fleming, Duffin, Forrest, Fraser, Hamilton, Shirra Shields, Walker, Donnelly,
Subs McFadyen, Ure, Carroll

Bo'ness started the game brightly with Shields, Donnelly and Shirra all coming close in the early stages, but it was to be the home side who took the lead after seventeen minutes, totally against the run of play. This didn't seem to downhearten the visitors, as they continued to dominate the game. They deservedly equalised in the twenty-eighth minute, Hamilton heading home a Fleming free kick, Shields was then unlucky when his goal bound shot was parried onto the bar. Before half-time Selkirk enjoyed their best spell of the match, with McGurk having to look lively to keep the game level at the interval.

Bo'ness were "quick off the blocks" at the start of the second half scoring two goals within a minute to put themselves well and truly in the driving seat. The first came in the forty-seventh minute, when Shields blasted home a tremendous effort from the edge of the box into the top corner of the net.

151

A minute later Forrest headed home number three. With sixty-four minutes on the clock the game was effectively over when Shirra drilled home a fourth. As the minutes ticked away substitute Ure grabbed a fifth with Shirra grabbing his second of the afternoon to complete a historic victory. To round off the day the Bo'ness players acknowledged the large travelling support who made their presence felt throughout the game.

Bo'ness' reward was a home tie against Third Division Queens Park. After a nervy start that saw the BU's go a goal behind after eight minutes, they soon got to grips with the game. It took until the last minute of the first half before they got their reward, when the referee pointed to the spot after an infringement in the box. Fleming converted the kick to level the game at the interval. In the second period a rejuvenated Bo'ness side pressed forward, looking for that all important second goal. It was not all one way traffic as the "Spiders",who had felt rather aggrieved at the penalty award, were also looking for that decisive second goal. As it turned out, with fifteen minutes remaining, a through ball by Fleming found Shields, who waltzed past a bemused Queen's Park defence before slotting the ball into the net. Queens Park tried in vain to salvage the tie ,but the Bo'ness defence stood firm, with keeper McGurk pulling off a fine save from close range as the minutes ticked away. When the final whistle sounded,a huge cheer went round the ground to cap one of the most memorable matches seen at Newtown Park for some time.

Highland League champions Buckie Thistle were next on the agenda at Newtown Park, as another large crowd gathered in hope of a victory which would put them in the hat along with Scotland's elite. As it turned out the home support were silenced after only five minutes on the clock, when the visitors took an early lead. Bo'ness enjoyed lengthy periods of possession, but failed to find the net. In the end Buckie double their lead in the fifty-seventh minute, there was to be no more goals. This was a hard one for Bo'ness to take as to contribute so much into the match and to leave getting nothing out of it left everyone involved bitterly disappointed.
Livingston crashed out of the competition at the first time of asking, against lower league Elgin City at Borough Briggs. Livingston started well and created numerous chances but failed to make any count. Just on the hour mark, Livingston paid the price for missed chances as the home side took the lead. Livingston went all out attack and were awarded a penalty after Craig Barr went down in the box, but after lengthy consultations between

152

referee and linesman the decision was overturned with Elgin being awarded a free kick instead. Livingston were not to be outdone. As they pressed forward, Russell lashed home the equaliser from a tight angle. Celebrations were short lived however, as barely three minutes later Elgin regained the lead. Livi keeper Bullock charged out of his box to clear a bouncing ball, but missed it completely, leaving Crooks the simple task of knocking the ball into the empty net to end Livingston's cup dreams for another season.

THE BIGGER PICTURE

Motherwell defeated St Johnstone 3-0, while Celtic knocked out Aberdeen 4-0. Celtic lifted the trophy in what was to be Neil Lennon's first season as manager with a 3-0 victory.

With Bo'ness United retaining the East Super League the club went into the first round draw for the 2011-12 season. Although drawn away to Fort William, Bo'ness were firm favourites to reach the next round and they didn't disappoint. A Scott Gibb double set them on their way, the first coming after fifteen minutes when he headed home a Nimmo corner.Seven minutes later Gibb added his second, again from the head, and from a Nimmo corner. Walker added a third for Bo'ness on the half hour mark. After the break Tarditi beat the Fort William keeper to a high ball before rolling it into the empty net and end the scoring.

The second round saw Whitehill Welfare visit Newtown Park. Bo'ness had to do without the services of striker John Stewart, the previous week in a match against St Andrews, Stewart lashed out in frustration after missing a chance and injured his foot in the result of kicking a wall. Luckily for him Tarditi carried on where he had finished off from the previous round. First of all he struck home a volley after seven minutes,and eleven minutes later Walker set him up to knock in an easy second goal. A seventy seventh minute penalty saw Welfare pull one back but despite heavy pressure United held out to progress into the third round.

A home tie for Bo'ness against Second Division leaders Cowdenbeath proved too much for the Junior side, which wasn't helped by the fact they were reduced to nine men. New signing Ryan Scanlon harshly saw red after only twenty-two minutes and this proved to be the turning point in the game . Up until that point Bo'ness had held their own in the early exchanges. With extra man advantage Cowdenbeath upped their game, and it was no surprise when they took the lead some fifteen minutes later.

Midway through the second half and the visitors doubled their lead. Bo'ness never gave up hope and had a strong penalty appeal waved away with six minutes remaining, when Nicky Walker went down in the box. To rub salt into Bo'ness wounds Cowdenbeath scored from the penalty spot just two minutes later, and to add further misery Hunter was sent off for kicking the ball at Coult the goalscorer as he celebrated. As the final whistle sounded the disgruntled home fans booed young ref Paul Robertson off at the end.

Livingston entering the Cup at the third round stage travelled down to Ayrshire to take on Junior side Irvine Meadow, a first competitive match for the club against a Junior side. 1,586 spectators crammed into the tiny Meadow Park, a potential "banana skin" was on the cards, but man of the match Marc McNulty had other ideas as he slammed home a first half hat-trick,. The first came in just six minutes and eased the nerves of the West Lothian side. Rory Boulding who like NcNulty proved to be a thorn in Irvine Meadows side all afternoon, grabbed a fourth before the half-time whistle. Deuchar then added a fifth for Livingston just into the second half, with Barr completing the rout with a sixth just on the final whistle.

Livingston once again were drawn against Ayrshire opposition, this time with a home draw against fellow First Division side Ayr United. Livingston, not playing to their best, still had the bulk of the first half but failed to make it count. As so often happens they found themselves a goal down when Ayr struck against the run of play with just over six minutes of the first half remaining. Just on the half-time whistle Livi's in-form Marc McNulty scored from close range, following a Fotheringham corner. If the Livingston fans thought this would be the turning point, then they were very much mistaken, as the Ayrshire men regained the lead within seven minutes of the restart. This proved to be the winner, as the only thing the home fans had to shout about was a penalty appeal when Russell was sent sprawling by the Ayr keeper. At the end of the day a very disappointing home defeat was capped by an equally poor home crowd of 932.

THE BIGGER PICTURE

Hibernian defeated Aberdeen, while capital rivals Heart of Midlothian defeated Celtic to set up the first Edinburgh final since 1896, Heart of Midlothian went on to lift the trophy with a superb 5-1 victory. Hearts sat back after the fifth goal was scored or the result could have been more damaging.

Moving into season 2012-13, and Livingston were drawn at home to Premier League strugglers Dundee. Any chance of a cup up-set were quickly dashed as the visitors found the net twice in the opening seventeen minutes, the second coming from the penalty spot. Things may have changed if Livingston were awarded their own penalty moments later, but the ref waved away Livingston's furious appeals when a Liam Fox effort seemed to have been handled before being cleared off the line. Dundee had chances to kill off the game before half-time, but failed to secure that crucial third goal. The second half was a different story however, as Livingston came more into the game as Tony Andreu and Burton O'Brien both tested Dundee's Rab Douglas. Late on Marc McNulty carved out a few chances, but it was not to be Livingston's day as they trundled out of the cup first time of asking.

THE BIGGER PICTURE

Hibernian defeated Falkirk 4-3 after extra time , an excellent fightback after being 3-0 down on the half hour mark. Celtic also needed extra time to see off Dundee United with the scoreline also ending up 4-3. Celtic had little difficulty disposing of Hibernian in the final, goals from Hooper (2) and Leadly sealing a 3-0 victory.

2013-14 Cup campaign once again saw Junior top dogs Linlithgow Rose enter the first round draw with a home tie against Highland League side Nairn County. The game was barely a minute old when the home side nearly snatched the lead, Colin Strictland just failing to finish off after a neat build-up. Linlithgow went ahead when a deep cross lead to Nairn's McIntosh heading into his own net. It took until the eighty fifth minute before the home side sealed victory, when a Steven Meechan volley to round of the day with a 2-0 victory. The second round saw Linlithgow travel North to Banff to take on Deveronvale. They were to end up paying the penalty as they threw away a two goal lead in the last ten minutes, after Smith and Coyne had the visitors on easy street. Long before the disastrous ten minute spell the game should have been all but sewn up, manager Bradley commenting after the match, that his side were not ruthless enough. As it turned out Linlithgow went down 3-1 in the replayed match at Prestonfield. The homesters started brightly enough when Calum Smith slammed home an early goal within five minutes. However what followed was a stop start match littered with fouls and poor refereeing decisions, as Deveronvale turned dirty. This seemed to unsettle Linlithgow, it was a clear game plan for the Highlanders and it worked a treat. Before half-time they were on level terms.

Rose started the second period more promising, but it was to be Deveronvale who were to take the lead with fifteen minutes remaining. The home side were desperately unlucky not to equalise moments later as the ball bobbled around the box. Coyne, Shirra and Strickland all failed to find the net in a goalmouth stramash. This was to prove costly as sub Herd accidently clashed off the ball and outside the box, remarkably the ref flashed a red card and pointed to the spot, Christie saved the resulting penalty kick but was unable to keep out the rebound which effectively finished the tie.

Linlithgow Rose v Nairn County © Mr.Donald L. Matheson (Nairn County)

Livingston travelled to MacDiarmid Park to take on St Johnstone and once again the Amondvale men stumbled at the first hurdle. The home side dominated the early stages of this match, but Livingston also created one or two chances, notably from Fordyce and McNult. However it was to be the home side that were to take the lead, midway through the first half when May hammered home from twenty yards. After the break the St Johnstone keeper came to the rescue for the homesters saving an angled drive from McNulty. Just after the hour mark, Livingston fell further behind, when the ball was bundled home from close range. Livingston kept battling to the end, and in the closing stages Fordyce and McNulty once again came close, with Simon Mensing hitting the bar with a looping header. In the end another gallant effort, but once again Premiership opposition proved too much for the Livingston men.

THE BIGGER PICTURE

Dundee United defeated Rangers 3-1, while St Johnstone reached the final with a 2-1 win over Aberdeen, both matches played at Ibrox. Over 47,000 saw St Johnstone lift their first major trophy in their 130 year history, with a 2-0 win at Celtic Park.

Linlithgow Rose automatically entered the Scottish Cup when they became members of the Scottish Football Association. In the first round, Linlithgow made the long trip up to Fraserburgh to kick off their Scottish Cup campaign. In a fairly evenly balanced game, both teams had chances to win the match, but in the end a 0-0 draw was a fair enough result. The replay at Preston field saw a more dominant Linlithgow Rose side, where early chances from Coyne and Kelbie all failed to find the net. Just past the half hour mark, and the visitors stunned the homesters by breaking the deadlock. Moments later a fine save from McKinven prevented Linlithgow Rose from going further behind and just before half time Coyne struck a deserved equaliser. Following the break, the visitors were down to ten men as a Fraserburgh defender denied a goal scoring opportunity pulling down Roddie McLennan. Rose were now firmly in control and took advantage of the extra man in the sixty-fifth minute when Coyne grabbed his second goal from a Blair Batchelor cross. "Broch" desperately tried to keep the tie alive, but Rose held off and went through to the next round.

Bo'ness marched comfortably into the second round with a 4-0 win over Lowland League side Selkirk at Yarrow Park. Bo'ness opened the scoring with a close range effort from Chris Donnelly. Selkirk's O'Connor had a couple of chances to get the home side back to level terms, but it was Bo'ness who were unlucky not to go 2 ahead in the twenty fifth minute, when Gribben's long range effort smashed off the bar. Murphy was on hand to put the ball in the net, but was judged offside. The second goal arrived just on the half hour mark, when Gribben headed home. Into the second half and Bo'ness continued to dominate producing many chances. With little more than ten minutes remaining, Bo'ness eventually wrapped up the tie when Gribbens scored his second, and Bo'ness' third. Five minutes later and the score was complete when Walker beat the advancing Selkirk keeper and passed to Pitman who had the easiest task and tapped into the empty goal.

Linlithgow were up against another Lowland league team Dalbeattie Star. Within ten minutes Tommy Coyne opened the scoring after being set up by Derek Sricktland. That turned out to be the only goal of the first half in which was a tightly contested cup tie. Within five minutes of the re-start McLennan doubled Roses lead, but within a couple of minutes, Star pegged back Rose' lead but before the visitors had time to regroup, Strickland volleyed home from close range within two minutes. Strickland was on the score sheet once again when his deflected shot found the back of the net to wrap up the tie. Just for good measure substitute Kelbie rounded off the scoring with another deflected goal a minute into stoppage time.

Bo'ness progressed into the third round with ease, as they hammered seven goals past Culter. The visitors surprised the Bo'ness faithful by scoring after three minutes, but that's as good as it got for Culter. A Donnelly hat-trick and a Gribben double had Bo'ness on easy streets before half time, but it took until the closing minutes before we saw the final scoring, Anderson 89 minutes and Walker 90 minutes completed the route.

The third round and Linlithgow Rose were rewarded against Championship side Raith Rovers. Colin Smith, Colin Strickland and Roddie McLennan all tested the visiting keeper McGurn who was on splendid form, to keep the game tied at half time. Sadly the hosts failed to find their early form and when defender Garry Thom impeded Stuart in the box, the referee had no hesitation but to point to the spot, and the Fifers made no mistake with the penalty. With five minutes remaining, Rovers secured the tie with a powerfully headed goal to round off the scoring. Linlithgow Rose 0 Raith Rovers 2.

Bo'ness were also rewarded with a league side, this time against Second Division strugglers Elgin City at Broughbriggs. Well before half time, City found themselves 3-0 up and as it stood, things did not look good for the visitors and their large travelling support. An inspirational second half substitution by the visitors saw Kieran Anderson and Nicky Walker come off the bench. Within seven minutes of the restart Anderson pulled one back after fine work from Pitman. Six minutes later and it was Walker's turn as he latched onto a Gribben's through ball to score Bo'ness' second. Within a minute Gribben equalised for Bo'ness to send the visiting support into a frenzy. Bo'ness pressed for the winner but it was to be the home side who regained the lead on the seventy two minute mark. Bo'ness were not to be outdone however, and with eight minutes remaining Scott scrambled the ball over the line to tie the scores 4-4 and earn a deserved replay at Newtown Park.

Yet another incredible game saw Bo'ness progress into the fourth round in a nine goal thriller. It took just three minutes for Gribben to find the net but within ten minutes the visitors were on level terms, scoring from the penalty spot. Snowden put Bo'ness back in front in the seventeenth minute heading home from an Anderson corner. Gribben notched his second and Bo'ness' third just after the half hour mark. The visitors should have pulled one back when they were awarded a second penalty, but this time around Peat kept the resulting kick out. Before half time however, Elgin pulled one back with the spot kick sinner Sutherland slotting home before half time; 3-2. More goals were to follow with Gribben's being judged offside for what would have been his hat-trick. However, Campbell made it four for Bo'ness in the fifty-sixth minute, again Elgin struck back in the seventy-second minute but Bo'ness kept pressing forward and found the net for the fifth time with Walker calmly striking the ball home with only a few minutes remaining. Ex- Rangers striker Marvin Andrews pulled another goal back for Elgin to set up a nervy finish, but at the end of the day Bo'ness deservedly went through in what was an amazing tie ending 5-4, and an incredible 17 goals scored in both matches.

Bo'ness United in action v Elgin City © George Sansom (Bo'ness United)

Livingston continued their dire run in the competition with an away defeat to lower league Annan Athletic. Although Livingston took an early lead after 13 minutes through Jacob's, the West Lothian outfit went in at the interval trailing 2-1 , and two goals coming from Weatherson in the 20th and 41st minutes . Just before the hour mark Annan increased their lead, which seemed to put the tie beyond doubt, however substitute Mullen managed to pull one back for Livingston with seven minutes remaining following a goalmouth scramble. The visitors threw everything   at Annan in the final minutes, but were unable to get that decisive third goal which would have forced a replay, indeed it was the home side who came closest , striking the bar in stoppage time.

The fourth round saw Bo'ness paired with another League Two side, this time around it was against table toppers Arbroath. Bo'ness started off brightly enough and were passing the ball around well, creating a good few chances, but it was to be Arbroath who were to take the lead in the twenty-seventh minute which turned out to be the only goal of the half.   The second period saw Bo'ness again start well, but were unable to find a breakthrough, but then in a disastrous eight minute spell starting in the sixty-eighth minute Arbroath doubled their lead and within a minute had made it three. Another quick double killed the tie in the seventy-fifth and seventy-sixth minutes. A late effort from Gribben failed to find the net and a consolation goal to end Bo'ness' Scottish Cup Campaign.

THE BIGGER PICTURE

Falkirk defeated Hibernian 1-0 while Inverness Caledonian Thistle beat Celtic 3-2 after extra time. Thistle went on to lift the trophy, for the first time in their short history, down to ten men the highlanders grabbed the winner with only four minutes remaining to secure a 2-1 victory.

THE COMPLETE SCOTTISH CUP & *QUALIFYING CUP* RECORDS FOR WEST LOTHIAN TEAMS

SCOTTISH CUP 1881- 82

1st Round
10th Sept   Hibernian 7 Addiewell 0
17th Sept   West Calder 5 Kinleith 1

2nd Round
1st Oct   West Calder W Dunfermline O

3rd Round
22nd Oct   West Calder 4 Brunswick 1

4th Round
19th Nov   West Calder W Stranraer O

5th Round
10th Dec   West Calder 4 Falkirk 2

6th Round
31st Dec   West Calder 3 Cartvale 5

SCOTTISH CUP 1882 - 83.

1st Round
9th Sept   Addiewell   W   Dunfermline O.
9th Sept   West Calder W   Kinleith   O.

2nd Round
7th Oct   West Calder 2 Hibernian 3.
7th Oct   Addiewell   0 Heart of Midlothian 14.

SCOTTISH CUP 1883 - 84.

1st Round
8th Sept   Hibernian 5 West Calder 0

SCOTTISH CUP 1884 - 85.

1st Round
13th Sept   Bo'ness FC 0 Hibernian 2
13th Sept   West Calder 3 Norton Park 0

2nd Round
4th Oct   West Calder 0 Dunblane 1

SCOTTISH CUP 1885-86.

1st Round
12th Sept   Broxburn Shamrock 1 Bo'ness FC 1
19th Sept   Bo'ness FC 5   Broxburn Shamrock 1
12th Sept   West Calder W Newcastleton O

2nd Round
3rd Oct   Bo'ness FC 8 Norton Park 1
          West Calder, Bye

3rd Round

24th Oct   Wishaw Swifts 3   West Calder 0
24th Oct   Hibernian 6 Bo'ness FC 0

SCOTTISH CUP   1886-87.

1st Round

11th Sept   West Calder 1   Armadale FC 3
11th Sept   Broxburn Shamrock 1   Mossend Swifts 2
11th Sept   Bellstane Birds 2 Broxburn Thistle 2
18th Sept   Broxburn Thistle 4   Bellstane Birds 1
11th Sept   St Bernards 3   Bo'ness FC 2
11th Sept   Hibernian 6 Durhamtown Rangers 1

2nd Round

2nd Oct   Broxburn Thistle 1   Heart of Midlothian 2
2nd Oct   Mossend Swifts 1 Hibernian 1
9th Oct   Hibernian 3 Mossend Swifts 0
2nd Oct   Newcastleton 1 Armadale FC 5

3rd Round

23rd Oct   St Bernards 5 Armadale FC 2

SCOTTISH CUP 1887 - 88.

1st Round

3rd Sept   Bo'ness FC 4 Leith Athletic 1
3rd Sept   Broxburn Shamrock 0 Mossend Swifts 4 (Mossend Disqualified)
3rd Sept   Erin Rovers 5 Bellstane Birds 0
3rd Sept   Hibernian 5 Broxburn Thistle 0
3rd Sept   St. Bernards 3 Armadale FC 2
3rd Sept   West Calder 9 Athenian 0

2nd Round

24th Sept   Bo'ness FC 5 West Calder 1
24th Sept   St. Bernards 1 Broxburn Shamrock 1
1st Oct   St. Bernards 4 Broxburn Shamrock 1
24th Sept   Erin Rovers 0 Hibernian 6

3rd Round
15th Oct   Lassodie 1 Bo'ness FC 3

4th Round
5th Nov   Vale of Leven Wanderers 2 Bo'ness FC 0

SCOTTISH CUP 1888-89.

1st Round
1st Sept   Armadale FC 12   Champfleurie 0
1st Sept   Bellstane Birds 2   Norton Park 3
1st Sept   Bo'ness FC 0   Heart of Midlothian 1
1st Sept   Broxburn Shamrock 3   West Calder 2
15th Sept West Calder 2   Broxburn Shamrock 1 (After Protest)
1st Sept   Erin Rovers 6   Leith H 0
1st Sept   Linlithgow Athletic 2   Adventurers 6
1st Sept   Mossend Swifts 2   Hibernian 1
          Broxburn F.C. Bye

2nd Round
22nd Sept   Broxburn F.C. 9   Adventurers 3
22nd Sept   West Calder 1   Mossend Swifts 6
22nd Sept   Heart of Midlothian 4   Erin Rovers 0
          Armadale FC , Bye

3rd Round
13th Oct   Broxburn FC. 2   Heart of Midlothian 2
20th Oct   Heart of Midlothian 2   Broxburn FC. 0
13th Oct   Mossend Swift 5   Armadale FC 2

4th Round
4th Nov   Uddingston 1   Mossend Swifts 4

5th Round
1st Dec   Dumbarton 3   Mossend Swifts 1

SCOTTISH CUP   1889-90.

1st Round
7th Sept   Armadale FC   2   Hibernian   3
7th Sept   Bathgate FC   3   Champfleurie   3
14th Sept Bathgate FC   O   Champfleurie   W
7th Sept   Bellstane Birds   6   Norton Park   3
7th Sept   Mossend Swifts   6   Bo'ness FC   0
7th Sept   West Calder   2   Broxburn F.C.   9

2nd Round
28th Sept Broxburn FC.   2   Leith Athletic   2
5th Oct   Leith Athletic   2   Broxburn FC.   1
28th Sept Bellstane Birds   1   Heart of Midlothian   4
28th Sept Hibernian   4   Mossend Swifts   3
              Champfleurie,   Bye

3rd Round
19th Oct   Champfleurie 0   Heart of Midlothian   5

SCOTTISH CUP   1890-91.

1st Round
6th Sept   Bathgate Rovers 3   Dunfermline Athletic   2
6th Sept   Bo'ness   W   Blair Adam   O
6th Sept   Broxburn FC.   W   West Calder   O
6th Sept   Leith Athletic 3   Armadale FC   2
6th Sept   Mossend Swifts   W   Lassodie   O
6th Sept   Penicuik Athletic 5   Champfleurie   3
6th Sept   Cowdenbeath   10   Linlithgow Athletic   1
              Bellstane Birds,   Bye

2nd Round
27th Sept   Bathgate Rovers 6   Union   2
27th Sept   Bo'ness FC   7   Bellstane Birds   0
27th Sept   Broxburn FC 5   Clackmannan   2
27th Sept   Jamestown 2   Mossend Swifts   5

3rd Round
18th Oct	Bathgate Rovers 6	Broxburn F.C. 0
18th Oct	Bo'ness FC 1	Mossend Swifts 1
25th Oct	Mossend Swifts 9	Bo'ness FC 1

4th Round
8th Nov	Dumbarton 7	Mossend Swifts 3
8th Nov	Abercorn 8	Bathgate Rovers 0

SCOTTISH CUP 1891-92.

1st Round - Preliminary
5th Sept	Broxburn FC 2	Raith Rovers 1
5th Sept	Armadale FC 3	Bathgate Rovers 3
12th Sept	Bathgate Rovers 3	Armadale FC 0
5th Sept	Dunfermline Athletic 4	Bo'ness FC 0
5th Sept	Muirhouse Rovers 1	Mossend Swifts 7
5th Sept	Burntisland T 4	Linlithgow Athletic 6
	Broxburn Shamrock W	Lochgelly United O

2nd Round - Preliminary
26th Sept	Bathgate Rovers 8	Slamannan 1
26th Sept	Alva 3	Mossend Swifts 9
26th Sept	Broxburn Shamrock 6	Campsie 4
3rd Oct	Broxburn Shamrock 3	Campsie 1 (After Protest)
26th Sept	Duntocher H 4	Broxburn F.C. 2
26th Sept	Smithston H 11	Linlithgow Athletic 1

3rd Round - Preliminary
17th Oct	Bathgate Rovers 5	Falkirk 5
24th Oct	Falkirk 0	Bathgate Rovers 3
17th Oct	East Stirlingshire 5	Mossend Swifts 4
17th Oct	Smithton H 1	Broxburn Shamrock 2

4th Round - Preliminary
7th Nov	Bathgate Rovers 5	Clydebank 1
	Broxburn Shamrock	Bye

1st Round

28th Nov Bathgate Rovers 6 Linthouse 0

28th Nov Broxburn Shamrock 7 Northern 2

2nd Round

19th Dec Broxburn Shamrock 4 Heart of Midlothian 5

19th Dec Queens Park 6 Bathgate Rovers 0

SCOTTISH CUP 1892-93.

1st Round Preliminary

Bathgate Rovers 7 Adventurers 1

Bo'ness FC 3 Polton Vale 4

Broxburn Shamrock 5 Bonnyrigg Rose 0

Mossend Swifts 2 Broxburn FC 1

Linlithgow Athletic 4 Muirhouse Rovers 1

Dunfermline Athletic 1 Armadale FC 4

2nd Round Preliminary

Broxburn Shamrock W Bridge of Allan O

Clackmannan 4 Armadale FC 3

Duntocher Harp 2 Mossend Swifts 1

Levendale 4 Bathgate Rovers 1

Linlithgow Athletic 3 Glairdoch 3

Glairdoch 6 Linlithgow Athletic 3

3rd Round Preliminary

Broxburn Shamrock 3 East Stirlingshire 1

4th Round Preliminary

Broxburn Shamrock 4 Partick Thistle 3

1st Round

26th Nov Dunblane 0 Broxburn Shamrock 3

2nd Round

17th Dec Broxburn Shamrock 3 Kings Park 0

168

3rd Round
21st Jan   Broxburn Shamrock 4 St. Mirren 3

Semi-Finals
18th Feb   Queens Park 4 Broxburn Shamrock 2

SCOTTISH CUP 1893-94.

1st Round - Preliminary
Armadale FC   8 First Argyll & Sutherland Highlanders 1
Bathgate FC   0 Kirkcaldy 0
Kirkcaldy 3 Bathgate FC   2
Bonnyrigg Rose 4 Bo'ness FC   3
Mossend Swifts 9 Adventurers 0
Lochgelly United   W   Linlithgow Athletic O
Polton Vale 5   Uphall FC   2
Broxburn FC.   Bye

2nd Round - Preliminary
Hibernian   5   Broxburn FC 0
Grangemouth 6   Armadale FC   2
Duntocher Harp 2   Mossend Swifts 5
3rd Round - Preliminary
Kirkcaldy 3   Mossend Swifts 3
Mossend Swifts   W Kirkcaldy O

4th Round - Preliminary
Mossend Swifts 2 Port Glasgow Athletic 2
Port Glasgow Athletic 9 Mossend Swifts 3

1st Round
25th Nov   Broxburn Shamrock 3 Arbroath 8

SCOTTISH CUP 1894-95.

1st Round - Preliminary
Bonnyrigg Rose 1 Bo'ness FC   4
Broxburn Shamrock 11 Loch Rangers 1
Kelso 0 Uphall FC   5

Linlithgow Athletic 4   Bathgate FC 1
Lochgelly United   1 Mossend Swifts 3

2nd Round - Preliminary
Camelon 3 Broxburn Shamrock 1
Linlithgow Athletic 2 Bo'ness FC 5
Mossend Swifts 2 Kilsyth Wanderers 0
Mossend Swifts 5 Kilsyth Wanderers 0 (After Protest)
Uphall FC 2 Raith Rovers 4

3rd Round - Preliminary
Clackmannan 1 Mossend Swifts 3
Bo'ness FC   Bye

4th Round - Preliminary
Ayr Parkhouse 2 Bo'ness FC 2
Bo'ness FC 1 Ayr Parkhouse 6
Mossend Swifts Bye

1st Round
24th Nov   Motherwell 1   Mossend Swifts 2

2nd Round
15th Dec   Ayr Parkhouse 3   Mossend Swifts 1

SCOTTISH QUALIFYING CUP 1895-96

1st Round
Bathgate FC 5   Linlithgow Athletic 0
Bo'ness FC W Kelso O
Uphall FC 2 Kirkcaldy 5
Mossend Swifts   Bye

2nd Round
Kings Park 3   Mossend Swifts 2
Kirkcaldy 4 Bo'ness FC 0
Stenhousemuir 7 Bathgate FC 0

170

SCOTTISH QUALIFYING CUP 1896-97

1st Round
Armadale Volunteers 3 Broxburn Shamrock 1
Bo'ness FC O Lochgelly W
Linlithgow Athletic O Penicuik Athletic W
Mossend Swifts 1 Raith Rovers 2
West Calder O Bathgate FC W

2nd Round
Bathgate FC W Selkirk O
Penicuik Athletic 4 Armadale Volunteers 0

3rd Round
Bathgate FC 6 Cameronians 2

4th Round
Bathgate FC (Bye)

5th Round
Bathgate FC (Bye)

6th Round
Orion 5 Bathgate FC 1

SCOTTISH CUP 1896-97

1ST Round
9th Jan   Blantyre 5 Bathgate 0

SCOTTISH QUALIFYING CUP 1897-98

1st Round
Bathgate 8 Vale of Leithen 1
Broxburn Shamrock 3 Selkirk 2
Mossend Swifts 1 Bo'ness 4
West Calder 4 Armadale Volunteers 0

171

2ⁿᵈ Round
Broxburn Shamrock O Bo'ness FC W
*Penicuik 3 West Calder 3 *(Penicuik awarded tie, see main text)*
Trinity O Bathgate FC W

3ʳᵈ Round
Bo'ness FC 1 Penicuik 0
Bathgate FC (Bye)

4ᵗʰ Round
Bo'ness FC 2 East Stirlingshire 6
Polton Vale 7 Bathgate FC 0

SCOTTISH CUP 1897-98

1ˢᵀ Round
8ᵗʰ Jan   Bo'ness FC 0 Queens Park 6
8ᵗʰ Jan   Cartvale 4 Bathgate FC 2

SCOTTISH QUALIFYING CUP - 1898-99

1ˢᵗ Round
Broxburn Shamrock O Vale of Leithen W
Penicuik 1 Bathgate FC 1
Penicuik 2 Bathgate FC 2
Penicuik 3 Bathgate FC 0
Polton Vale 4 Armadale Volunteers 1
Selkirk O Bo'ness FC W
West Calder 8 Mossend Swifts 1

2ⁿᵈ Round
Adventurers 0 Bo'ness FC 3
West Calder W Vale of Leithen O

3ʳᵈ Round
Bo'ness FC 3 Polton Vale 2
Clackmannan 1 West Calder 2

172

4ᵗʰ Round
Bo'ness FC (Bye)
West Calder (Bye)

5ᵗʰ Round
Bo'ness FC 3 Forfar Athletic 2
East Stirlingshire 3 West Calder 1

6ᵗʰ Round
Arbroath 2 Bo'ness FC 2
Bo'ness FC 1 Arbroath 2

SCOTTISH CUP 1898-99

1ˢᵗ Round
14ᵗʰ Jan   Bo'ness FC 3 St. Bernards 3
21ˢᵗ Jan   St. Bernards 4 Bo'ness FC 2
14ᵗʰ Jan   Forfar Athletic 4 West Calder 5

2ⁿᵈ Round
4ᵗʰ Feb   Port Glasgow Athletic 3 West Calder 1

SCOTTISH QUALIFYING CUP 1899-1900

1ˢᵗ Round
Armadale Volunteers O Mossend Swifts W
Bo'ness FC 5 Bathgate FC 1
West Calder 7 Vale of Leithen 1

2ⁿᵈ Round
Cowdenbeath 2 Mossend Swifts 0
Raith Rovers 1 West Calder 0
Selkirk 1 Bo'ness FC 1
Bo'ness FC 4 Selkirk 0

3ʳᵈ Round
Bo'ness FC 5 Hearts of Beath 2

4th Round
Bo'ness FC 2 Raith Rovers 2
Raith Rovers 3 Bo'ness FC 1

SCOTTISH CUP 1899-00

1st Round
13th Jan   Celtic 7 Bo'ness FC 1

SCOTTISH QUALIFYING CUP 1900-1901

1st Round
Bo'ness FC W Adventurers O
Mossend Swifts 3 Bathgate FC 0
Polton Vale O West Calder W

2nd Round
Mossend Swifts W Vale of Leithen O
West Calder 0 Bo'ness FC 3

3rd Round
Bo'ness FC W Edinburgh University O
Mossend Swifts (Bye)

4th Round
East Stirlingshire 1 Bo'ness FC 1
Bo'ness FC 0   East Stirlingshire 3
Mossend Swifts 2 Stenhousemuir 2
Stenhousemuir 2 Mossend Swifts 2
Mossend Swifts 1 Stenhousemuir 5

SCOTTISH CUP 1900-01

1st Round
12th Jan   Heart of Midlothian 7 Mossend Swifts 0
12th Jan   Morton 10 Bo'ness FC 0

174

SCOTTISH QUALIFYING CUP 1901-1902

1st Round
Bathgate FC 3 Bo'ness FC 3
Bo'ness FC 1 Bathgate FC 1
Bathgate FC 1 Bo'ness FC 2
Polton Vale O Mossend Swifts W
West Calder 3 Leith Athletic 0
East Benhar Rangers 2 Dykehead 4

2nd Round
Cowdenbeath 3 Bo'ness FC 1
Lochgelly 2 Mossend Swifts 1
Raith Rovers 6 West Calder 1

SCOTTISH QUALIFYING CUP 1902-03

1st Round
Bo'ness FC 4 Adventurers 3
Mossend Swifts 0 Broxburn F.C. 7
West Calder 3 Bathgate FC 5

2nd Round
Bathgate FC 1 Bo'ness FC 1
Bo'ness FC 2 Bathgate FC 3
Broxburn F.C. W Selkirk O

3rd Round
Bathgate FC 2 Broxburn FC 1
Broxburn FC 8 Bathgate FC 3 *(After Protest)*

4th Round
Stenhousemuir 2 Broxburn FC 1

SCOTTISH CUP 1902-03

1st Round
17th Jan   Leith Athletic 4 Broxburn FC 1

SCOTTISH QUALIFYING CUP 1903-04

1st Round
Black Watch 3 Bathgate FC 5
Bo'ness FC 10 Selkirk 1
West Calder Swifts 7 Adventurers 0
Broxburn FC (Bye)

2nd Round
Broxburn FC 3 Bathgate FC 2
Bathgate FC 2 Broxburn FC1   (After Protest)
West Calder Swifts 2 Bo'ness FC 1
3rd Round
Bathgate FC 1 West Calder Swifts 3

4th Round
West Calder Swifts 2 Hearts of Beith 1
Hearts of Beath 3 West Calder Swifts 5 (After Protest)

5th Round
West Calder Swifts 1 Arbroath 1
Arbroath 2 West Calder Swifts 0

SCOTTISH CUP 1903-04

1st Round
23rd Jan   St. Bernards 1 West Calder Swifts 1
30th Jan   West Calder Swifts 3 St. Bernards 3
6th Feb   St. Bernards 2 West Calder Swifts 0

SCOTTISH QUALIFYING CUP 1904-05

1st Round
Bathgate FC 3 Broxburn Shamrock 1
Bo'ness FC 1 Adventurers 1
Adventurers 2 Bo'ness FC 5
Leith Athletic 1 Broxburn FC 0
West Calder Swifts (Bye)

176

2nd Round
Bo'ness FC 0 Leith Athletic 2
Newcastleton O Bathgate FC W
West Calder Swifts 1 St. Bernards 1
St. Bernards 3 West Calder Swifts 1

3rd Round
Bathgate FC (Bye)

4th Round
Kirkcaldy United. 0 Bathgate FC 2

5th Round
Bathgate FC (Bye)

6th Round
Clyde 2 Bathgate FC 0

SCOTTISH CUP 1904-05

1st Round
28th Jan   Bathgate FC 2 Arbroath 1

2nd Round
18th Feb   Aberdeen 6 Bathgate FC 1

SCOTTISH QUALIFYING CUP 1905-06

1st Round
Bo'ness 5 Broxburn Athletic 0
Broxburn F.C. 1 Leith Athletic 1
Leith Athletic 2 Broxburn F.C. 0
Broxburn Shamrock 4 Adventurers 1
Broxburn Shamrock 3 Adventurers 2 (After Protest)
St. Bernards 4 Bathgate 2
West Calder Swifts 3 Berwick Rangers 3
Berwick Rangers 2 West Calder Swifts 1

2nd Round
Berwick Rangers 1 Bo'ness 2
Broxburn Shamrock 7 Selkirk 0
3rd Round
Bo'ness 3 Broxburn Shamrock 0

4th Round
Hamilton Academicals 3 Bo'ness 1

SCOTTISH CUP 1905-06

1st Round
27th Jan   Arbroath 1 Bo'ness 4
2nd Round
10th Feb   Celtic 3 Bo'ness 0

SCOTTISH QUALIFYING CUP 1906-07

1st Round
Bathgate 5   Berwick Rangers 1
Bo'ness 0   Broxburn Athletic 0
Broxburn Athletic 3   Bo'ness 2
Broxburn Shamrock 1   St. Bernards 1
St. Bernards 4   Broxburn Shamrock 0
Leith Athletic 3 Broxburn F.C. 0
West Calder Swifts 1   West Lothian Albion 4

2nd Round
Bathgate 2   Royal Garrison Artillery 0
Broxburn Athletic 0   St. Bernards 5
West Lothian Albion 0   Leith Athletic 2

3rd Round
Cowdenbeath 2 Bathgate 2
Bathgate 1   Cowdenbeath 1
Bathgate 0   Cowdenbeath 1

SCOTTISH QUALIFYING CUP 1907-08

1st Round
Bo'ness 1   Bathgate 1
Bathgate 0   Bo'ness 2
Broxburn Athletic 1   Broxburn F.C. 1
Broxburn F.C. 0   Broxburn Athletic 1
Uphall 0   Broxburn Shamrock 0
Broxburn Shamrock 2   Uphall 3
West Lothian Albion 0   Leith Athletic 2
West Calder Swifts (Bye)

2nd Round
Clackmannan 3 Uphall 3
Uphall 2   Clackmannan 1
Cowdenbeath 0 Bo'ness 0
Bo'ness 2   Cowdenbeath 0
St. Bernards 1   Broxburn Athletic 0
Stenhousemuir 1   West Calder Swifts 4

3rd Round
Bo'ness 2   Alloa Athletic 1
Elgin City 2   West Calder Swifts 1
Uphall 3   Aberdeen University 0

4th Round
Ayr Parkhouse 1   Bo'ness 1
Bo'ness 3   Ayr Parkhouse 1
Dumfries 3   Uphall 1

5th Round
Dumfries 3   Bo'ness 1

SCOTTISH CUP 1907 08

1st Round
18th Jan   Galston 6   Uphall 0
25th Jan   Partick Thistle 4   Bo'ness 0

179

SCOTTISH QUALIFYING CUP 1908-09

1st Round
Broxburn FC 3   Uphall 0
Broxburn Athletic 2   Bo'ness 0
Leith Athletic 2   Bathgate 0
St Bernards 5 West Lothian Albion 1
West Calder Swifts   Bye

2nd Round
Broxburn FC 1   Raith Rovers 0
West Calder Swifts 2 Broxburn Athletic 1

3rd Round
West Calder Swifts 2   Dunfermline Athletic 1
Broxburn FC   Bye

4th Round
Broxburn FC 2   Leith Athletic 2
Leith Athletic 3   Broxburn FC 1
West Calder Swifts 2 Elgin City 1

5th Round
Brechin City 0 West Calder Swifts 0
West Calder Swifts 0 Brechin City 2

SCOTTISH CUP   1908-09

1st Round
23rd Jan   Broxburn FC 1   Beith 1
30th Jan   Beith 0   Broxburn FC 0
3rd Feb   Broxburn FC 1   Beith 1
4th Feb   Beith 1   Broxburn FC 1
5th Feb   Broxburn FC 2   Beith 4
23rd Jan   West Calder Swifts 0   Partick Thistle 0
               Partick Thistle W   West Calder Swifts O

180

SCOTTISH QUALIFYING CUP 1909-10

1st Round
Bathgate FC 3 West Lothian Albion 0
Bo'ness FC 3 West Calder Swifts 0
Broxburn Athletic 1 St Bernards 3
Broxburn Shamrock 0 Leith Athletic 5
Broxburn FC Bye

2nd Round
Bathgate FC 2 East Stirlingshire 1
Bo'ness FC 3 Stenhousemuir 2
Bo'ness FC 2 Stenhousemuir 1 *(After Protest)*
Broxburn FC 1 East Fife 2

3rd Round
Bathgate FC Bye
Bo'ness FC Bye

4th Round
Bo'ness FC 0 Dumbarton FC 1
Partick Thistle 1 Bathgate FC 2

5th Round
Bathgate FC 1 Kirkcaldy United 1
Kirkcaldy United 1 Bathgate FC 3

Semi-Final
Bathgate FC 1 Dumbarton 0

Final
Leith Athletic 4 Bathgate FC 0

SCOTTISH CUP 1909-10

1st Round
22nd Jan   Bathgate FC 0   Heart of Midlothian 4
5th Feb   Aberdeen 3   Bo'ness FC 0

SCOTTISH QUALIFYING CUP 1910-11

1ˢᵗ Round
Armadale FC 1   Broxburn Shamrock 1

Broxburn Shamrock 2   Armadale FC 2
Armadale FC 5   Broxburn Shamrock 0
Bo'ness FC 3   West Calder Swifts 0
Leith Athletic 0   Bathgate FC 0
Bathgate FC 1   Leith Athletic 0 (Protested)
Bathgate FC 1   Leith Athletic 1
Leith Athletic 2   Bathgate FC 0
West Lothian Albion 0   Broxburn FC 0
Broxburn FC 1   West Lothian Albion 1
West Lothian Albion 1   Broxburn FC 4
St Bernards 4   Broxburn Athletic 0

2ⁿᵈ Round
Broxburn FC 1   Peebles Rovers 3
Bo'ness FC 5   Vale of Leithen 0
Leith Athletic 2   Armadale FC 0

3ʳᵈ Round
Bo'ness FC 2   Peebles Rovers 1 (Protested)
Bo'ness FC 1   Peebles Rovers 0

4ᵗʰ Round
Lochgelly United 1   Bo'ness FC 0

SCOTTISH CUP 1910-11

1ˢᵗ Round
28ᵗʰ Jan   Airdrieonians 2   Bo'ness FC 0

SCOTTISH QUALIFYING CUP 1911-12

1st Round
Armadale 4 West Lothian Albion 1
Bo'ness 1 Bathgate 6
Leith Athletic 1 Broxburn FC 0
St Bernards 4 Broxburn Shamrock 0
West Calder Swifts 5 Broxburn Athletic 0 (Protested)
West Calder Swifts 0 Broxburn Athletic 0
Broxburn Athletic 1 West Calder Swifts 0

2nd Round
Bathgate FC 1 St Bernards 1
St Bernards 1 Bathgate FC 3
Broxburn Athletic 0 Peebles 2 (Protested)
Broxburn Athletic 1 Peebles 0
Duns 0 Armadale FC 10

3rd Round
Broxburn Athletic 2 Gala Fairydean 1
Bathgate FC 1 Armadale FC 2

4th Round
Broxburn Athletic 1 Leith Athletic 2
Armadale FC 1 East Stirlingshire 1
East Stirlingshire 0 Armadale FC 0
Armadale FC 0 East Stirlingshire 0
East Stirlingshire 2 Armadale FC 0

SCOTTISH CUP 1911-12

1st Round
27th Jan   Broxburn Athletic 6 Beith FC 0
3rd Feb   Armadale 2 Peterhead 1

2nd Round
10th Feb   Third Lanark 6 Broxburn Athletic 1
17th Feb   Aberdeen 3 Armadale FC 0

183

SCOTTISH QUALIFYING CUP 1912-13

1st Round
Armadale FC 3   Musselburgh 1
Black Watch 1   West Calder Swifts 8
Broxburn United 2   Bo'ness FC 0
Leith Athletic 6   Broxburn Shamrock 0
West Lothian Albion O   Bathgate FC W

2nd Round
Bathgate FC 1   St Bernards 2
Broxburn United 1   West Calder Swifts 0
Gala Fairydean 1   Armadale FC 0

3rd Round
Broxburn United   Bye

4th Round
Broxburn United 0   Dundee Hibernian 1

SCOTTISH CUP 1912-13

1st Round
Broxburn United   Bye

2nd Round
8th Feb   Raith Rovers 5   Broxburn United 0

SCOTTISH QUALIFYING CUP 1913-14

1st Round
Armadale 1   St Bernards 1
St Bernards 1   Armadale 0
Bo'ness FC 2   Bathgate FC 3
Broxburn Shamrock 0   Leith Athletic 0
Leith Athletic 3   Broxburn Shamrock 0
West Calder Swifts O   Leith Amateurs W
Broxburn United   Bye

184

2nd Round
Bathgate FC 0   Broxburn United 1

3rd Round
Berwick Rangers 0   Broxburn United 3

4th Round
Kirkcaldy United 1   Broxburn United 0

SCOTTISH CUP 1913 -14
1st Round
Broxburn United   Bye

2nd Round
7th Feb   Broxburn United 5   Dumfries 1

3rd Round
21st Feb   Broxburn United 0   Motherwell 2

SCOTTISH QUALIFYING CUP 1914-15

1st Round
Broxburn Shamrock 1   Bo'ness FC 4
Broxburn United 1   Leith Amateurs 1
Leith Amateurs 1   Broxburn United 3
Leith Athletic 3   Bathgate FC 1
West Calder Swifts 1   Armadale FC 3

2nd Round
Armadale FC 2   Leith Athletic 0
Broxburn United W   Vale of Leithen O
Gala Fairydean 2   Bo'ness FC 1

3rd Round
Armadale FC   Bye
Broxburn United   Bye

4th Round
Broxburn United 3 Galafairydean 0
Armadale Bye

5th Round
Broxburn United 0 St Bernards 0
St Bernards 4 Broxburn United 0
Galston 3 Armadale FC 0

No *Qualifying* / Scottish Cup 1915-16
No *Qualifying* / Scottish Cup 1916-17
No *Qualifying* / Scottish Cup 1917-18
No *Qualifying* / Scottish Cup 1918-19

SCOTTISH QUALIFYING CUP 1919-20

1st Round
Armadale FC 1 Broxburn United 1
Broxburn United 1 Armadale 2
Bathgate FC 1 St Bernards 0
Bo'ness FC 7 Leith Amateurs 0

2nd Round
Armadale FC 6 Peebles Rovers 2
Gala Fairydean 0 Bo'ness FC 1
Bathgate FC Bye

3rd Round
Bathgate FC 2 Bo'ness FC 0
Armadale FC Bye
4th Round
Armadale FC Bye
Bathgate FC Bye

5th Round
Bathgate FC 4 St Johnstone 1
Inverness Caledonian 0 Armadale FC 1

6th Round
Bathgate FC 6   Arbroath 1
Cowdenbeath 2 Armadale FC 1

Semi-final
Bathgate FC 1   Vale of Leven 0

Final
Bathgate FC 2   Cowdenbeath 0

SCOTTISH CUP 1919-20

1st Round
24th Jan   Armadale FC 1   Clyde 0
24th Jan   Bathgate FC 0   St Bernards 2
24th Jan   Broxburn United   Bye

2nd Round
7th Feb   Armadale FC 1   Hibernian 0
7th Feb   Broxburn United 1   Queen of the South 0

3rd Round
21st Feb   Armadale FC 1 Ayr United 1
28th Feb   Ayr United 0   Armadale FC 1
21st Feb   Rangers 3   Broxburn United 0
4th Round
6th Mar   Armadale 1   Kilmarnock 2

SCOTTISH QUALIYFING CUP 1920-21

1st Round
Armadale FC 3   St Bernards 0
Bo'ness FC 6   Leith Athletic 0
Broxburn United 1 Bathgate FC 0

2nd Round
Berwick Rangers 1 Armadale FC 3
Bo'ness FC 5   Gala Fairydean 0
Broxburn United   Bye

3rd Round
Broxburn United 2   Peebles Rovers 0
Armadale FC   Bye
Bo'ness FC   Bye

4th Round
Alloa Athletic 1   Broxburn United 0
Armadale FC 2   Stenhousemuir 1
Bo'ness FC   Bye

5th Round
Alloa Athletic 2   Armadale FC 0
Bo'ness FC 2   Arbroath 1

6th Round
Bo'ness FC 2   East Stirlingshire 0

Semi-final
Bo'ness FC 1   Stevenston United 0

Final
East Fife 3   Bo'ness FC 1

SCOTTISH CUP 1920-21

1st Round
22nd Jan   Bo'ness FC 1   Galston 0
22nd Jan   St Mirren 2   Armadale FC 3
            Broxburn United   Bye

2nd Round
5th Feb   Bo'ness FC 0   Armadale FC 0
12th Feb   Armadale FC 2   Bo'ness FC 0
5th Feb   Broxburn United 1   Hamilton Academicals 2

3rd Round
19th Feb   Armadale FC 2   Albion Rovers 2
26th Feb   Albion Rovers 0   Armadale FC 0
2nd Mar   Armadale FC 0   Albion Rovers 0
3rd Mar   Albion Rovers 2   Armadale FC 0

188

SCOTTISH CUP 1921-22

1st Round
28th Jan Bathgate FC 3 Helensburgh 2
28th Jan Bo'ness 6 Stranraer 0
28th Jan Dundee Hibernian 0 Broxburn United 2
28th Jan Hibernian 3 Armadale FC 0

2nd Round
11th Feb Bathgate FC 1 Falkirk 0
11th Feb Clyde 5 Bo'ness FC 1
11th Feb Heart of Midlothian 2 Broxburn United 2
15th Feb Heart of Midlothian 2 Broxburn United 2
20th Feb Heart of Midlothian 3 Broxburn United 1

3rd Round
25th Feb Partick Thistle 3 Bathgate FC 0

SCOTTISH CUP 1922-23

1st Round
13th Jan Bo'ness 6 Clachnacuddin 0
13th Jan East Stirlingshire 1 Bathgate FC 1
17th Jan Bathgate FC 3 East Stirlingshire 2
13th Jan Johnstone 2 Armadale FC 0
13th Jan Kilmarnock 5 Broxburn United 0

2nd Round
27th Jan Bo'ness FC 3 Heart of Midlothian 2
27th Jan Queens Park 1 Bathgate FC 1
31st Jan Bathgate FC 0 Queens Park 2

3rd Round
10th Feb Bo'ness FC 2 Nithsdale Wanderers 0

4th Round
24th Feb Motherwell 4 Bo'ness FC 2

SCOTTISH CUP 1923-24

1st Round
26th Jan Bathgate FC 1   Bo'ness FC 1
30th Jan Bo'ness FC 1   Bathgate FC 0
26th Jan Coldstream 0   Armadale FC 1

26th Jan Raith Rovers 3   Broxburn United 0

2nd Round
9th Feb Partick Thistle 3   Bo'ness FC 0
9th Feb Queens Park 3   Armadale FC 1

SCOTTISH CUP 1924-25

1st Round
24th Jan Armadale FC 3   Civil Service 1
24th Jan Bathgate FC 0   Partick Thistle 4
24th Jan Bo'ness FC 1   Helensburgh 1
28th Jan Helensburgh 0   Bo'ness FC 0
3rd Feb Bo'ness FC 2   Helensburgh 0
24th Jan Broxburn United 3   Nithsdale Wanderers 2

2nd Round
7th Feb Armadale FC 1   Aberdeen 1
11th Feb Aberdeen 2   Armadale FC 0
7th Feb Raith Rovers 0   Bo'ness FC 0
11th Feb Bo'ness FC 1   Raith Rovers 3
7th Feb Royal Albert 1   Broxburn United 3

3rd Round
21st Feb Broxburn United 2   Falkirk 1

4th Round
7th Mar Dundee 1   Broxburn United 0

SCOTTISH CUP   1925-26

1st Round
23rd Jan Arthurlie 5   Armadale FC 4
23rd Jan Bathgate FC 5   East Stirlingshire 4
23rd Jan Bo'ness FC 2   East Fife 1
23rd Jan Hibernian 1   Broxburn United 1
26th Jan Hibernian 1   Broxburn United 0

2nd Round
6th Feb Bo'ness FC 1   Bathgate FC 1
10th Feb Bathgate FC 3   Bo'ness FC 1

3rd Round
20th Feb Bathgate FC 2   Airdrieonians 5

SCOTTISH QUALIFYING CUP   1926-27

1st Round
Leith Amateurs 1   Broxburn United 2

2nd Round
Civil Service Strollers 0   Broxburn United 1

3rd Round
Vale of Leithen 2   Broxburn United 5

4th Round
Broxburn United 4   Peebles Rovers 3

5th Round
Inverness Caledonian 3   Broxburn United 1

SCOTTISH CUP 1926-27

1st Round
22nd Jan Bathgate FC 2   Dunfermline Athletic 2
26th Jan Dunfermline Athletic 5   Bathgate FC 2
22nd Jan Bo'ness FC 3   Lochgelly United 0
22nd Jan Broxburn United 2   Armadale FC 1

2nd Round
5th Feb Bo'ness FC 2   Cowdenbeath 1
12th Feb Broxburn United 2   Montrose 2
16th Feb Montrose 1   Broxburn United 0

3rd Round
19th Feb Buckie Thistle 0   Bo'ness FC 3

4th Round
5th Mar Bo'ness FC 2   Celtic 5

SCOTTISH CUP 1927-28

1st Round
21st Jan Armadale FC 3   Berwick Rangers 1
21st Jan Ayr United 2   Bo'ness FC 0
21st Jan Celtic 3   Bathgate FC 1

2nd Round
4th Feb Armadale FC 2   Kings Park 4

SCOTTISH CUP 1928-29

1st Round
19th Jan Armadale FC 9   Moor Park 2
19th Jan Bo'ness FC 7   Newton Stewart 1
19th Jan St Andrews University 0   Bathgate FC 3
2nd Round
2nd Feb Ayr United 5   Armadale FC 1
2nd Feb Bathgate FC 1   Raith Rovers 1
6th Feb Raith Rovers 5   Bathgate FC 2
2nd Feb Kilmarnock 3   Bo'ness FC 2

SCOTTISH QUALIFYING CUP 1929-30

1st Round
Bathgate FC 4 Peebles Rovers 4
Peebles Rovers 1 Bathgate FC 3

192

2nd Round
Bathgate FC 5 Duns 1

3rd Round
Murrayfield Amateurs 0 Bathgate FC 1

4th Round
Bathgate FC 3 Vale of Leithen 1

5th Round
Civil Service Strollers 1 Bathgate FC 2

Semi-final
Inverness Citadel 1 Bathgate FC 1
Bathgate FC 1 Inverness Citadel 0

Final
7th Dec Bathgate FC 1 St Cuthberts Wanderers 0

SCOTTISH CUP 1929-30

1st Round
18th Jan Bo'ness FC 0 St Johnstone 0
22nd Jan St Johnstone 3 Bo'ness FC 1
18th Jan Inverness Citadel 1 Armadale FC 0
18th Jan Kings Park 6 Bathgate FC 2

SCOTTISH QUALIFYING CUP 1930/31

1st Round
Coldstream 2 Bathgate FC 4

2nd Round
Leith Amateurs 1 Bathgate FC 3

3rd Round
Bathgate FC 3 Peebles Rovers 2

4th Round
Bathgate FC 4   Civil Service Strollers 0

5th Round
Falkirk Amateurs 2   Bathgate FC 5

Semi Final
Bathgate FC 5   Buckie Thistle 0 (Protest)
Bathgate FC 3   Buckie Thistle 1

Final
13th Dec Bathgate FC 1   Dalbeattie Star 1
20th Dec Bathgate FC 1   Dalbeattie Star 0

SCOTTISH CUP 1930/31

1st Round
17th Jan Armadale FC 1   Rangers 7
17th Jan Bo'ness FC 3   Peterhead 0
17th Jan Motherwell 6   Bathgate FC 0

2nd Round
4th Feb Bo'ness FC 4   Alloa Athletic 2

3rd Round
14th Feb Bo'ness FC 1   Ayr United 0

4th Round
28th Feb Bo'ness FC 1   Kilmarnock 1
4th Mar Kilmarnock 5   Bo'ness FC 0

SCOTTISH QUALIFYING CUP 1931/32

1st Round
Leith Amateurs 3   Bathgate FC 1

SCOTTISH CUP

1st Round
16th Jan Armadale FC 3   Montrose 1
16th Jan Dalbeattie Star 2   Bo'ness FC 3

2nd Round
30th Jan Bo'ness FC 2   Partick Thistle 2
3rd Feb Partick Thistle 5   Bo'ness FC 1
30th Feb Hamilton Academicals 5   Armadale FC 2

SCOTTISH QUALIFYING CUP 1932/33

1st Round
Leith Amateurs W   Bathgate FC O

SCOTTISH CUP 1932/33

1st Round
21st Jan Armadale FC 0   Dundee United 2
21st Jan Stranraer 1   Bo'ness FC 1
28th Jan Bo'ness FC 3   Stranraer 0

2nd Round
1st Feb Dundee 4   Bo'ness FC 0

SCOTTISH QUALIFYING CUP 1933/34

1st Round
Armadale FC O   Civil Service Strollers W
Selkirk 3   Bo'ness FC 0
Broxburn St Johns   Bye

2nd Round
Edinburgh Uni O Broxburn St Johns W

3rd Round
Broxburn St Johns 1   Vale of Leithen 7

SCOTTISH QUALIFYING CUP 1934/35

1ˢᵗ Round
Bo'ness FC 3 Gala Fairydean 0

2ⁿᵈ Round
Edinburgh University 0 Bo'ness FC W

3ʳᵈ Round
Bo'ness FC 0 Berwick Rangers 0
Berwick Rangers 0 Bo'ness FC 5

Semi Finals
Bo'ness FC 4 Peebles Rovers 2

Final
3ʳᵈ Nov Beith 1 Bo'ness FC 1
10ᵗʰ Nov Beith 2 Bo'ness FC 1

SCOTTISH CUP 1934/35

1ˢᵗ Round
26ᵗʰ Jan Morton 9 Bo'ness FC 0

SCOTTISH QUALIFYING CUP 1935/36

1ˢᵗ Round
Bo'ness FC 3 Vale of Leithen 1

2ⁿᵈ Round
Penicuik Athletic 2 Bo'ness FC 2
Bo'ness FC 4 Penicuik 0

3ʳᵈ Round
Bo'ness FC 3 Chirnside 1

Semi Final
Bo'ness FC 7 Peebles Rovers 2

Final
2nd Nov Bo'ness FC 0 Galston 4

SCOTTISH CUP 1935/36

1st Round
1st Feb Bo'ness FC 1 Airdrieonians 3

SCOTTISH QUALIFYING CUP 1936/37

1st Round
Bo'ness FC 8 Coldstream 0

2nd Round
Bo'ness FC 5 Gala Fairydean 0

3rd Round
Bo'ness FC 3 Peebles Rovers 0

Semi-final
Duns 2 Bo'ness FC 1

SCOTTISH CUP 1936-37

1st Round
30th Jan Bo'ness FC 0 Cowdenbeath 6

SCOTTISH QUALIFYING CUP 1937- 38

1st Round
Bo'ness FC 3 Duns 3
Duns 0 Bo'ness FC 1

2nd Round
Murrayfield Amateurs 1 Bo'ness FC 4

3rd Round
Penicuik Athletic 2   Bo'ness FC 2
Bo'ness FC 4   Penicuik Athletic 2

Semi- final
Bo'ness FC 3   Vale of Leithen 1

Final
6th Nov Stranraer 5 Bo'ness FC 3

SCOTTISH CUP   1937-38

1st Round
22nd Jan Bo'ness FC 0   Hamilton Academicals 4

SCOTTISH QUALIFYING CUP 1938-39

1st Round
Bo'ness FC 4   Chirnside United 1

2nd Round
Selkirk 0   Bo'ness FC 2

3rd Round
Berwick Rangers 3   Bo'ness FC 2

SCOTTISH CUP 1938-39

1st Round
21st Jan Bo'ness FC 1   Hamilton Academicals 4

SCOTTISH CUP/ QUALIFYING CUP
Competitions suspended 1939-40 till 1945-46

SCOTTISH QUALIFYING CUP 1946-47

1st Round
Coldstream W Bo'ness FC O

No West Lothian teams from 1947 till 1995 in both cup competitions

SCOTTISH CUP 1995-96

1st Round
Stranraer 0   Livingston FC 3

2nd Round
Inverness Caledonian Thistle 3   Livingston FC 2
SCOTTISH CUP 1996-97

1st Round
Livingston FC   Bye

2nd Round
Brechin City 2   Livingston FC 1

SCOTTISH CUP 1997-98

1st Round
Livingston FC   Bye

2nd Round
Livingston FC 2   Berwick Rangers 1

3rd Round
Livingston FC 3   Albion Rovers 3
Albion Rovers 0   Livingston FC 0   (Albion Rovers win 6-5 on penalties)

SCOTTISH CUP 1998-99

1st Round
Dumbarton 1   Livingston FC 1
Livingston FC 3   Dumbarton 0

2nd Round
Inverness Caledonian Thistle 1   Livingston FC 2

3rd Round
Aberdeen 0   Livingston 1

4th Round
Livingston FC 1   St Johnstone 3

SCOTTISH CUP 1999-2000

1st Round
Livingston FC   Bye

2nd Round
Livingston FC   Bye

3rd Round
Queen of the South 0   Livingston FC 7

4th Round
Partick Thistle 2   Livingston FC 1

SCOTTISH CUP 2000-01

1st Round
Livingston FC   Bye

2nd Round
Livingston FC   Bye

3rd Round
East Fife 1   Livingston FC 4

4th Round
Livingston FC 0   Aberdeen 0
Aberdeen 0   Livingston FC 1

5th Round
Livingston FC 3   Peterhead 1

Semi-finals
Hibernian 3 Livingston FC 0

SCOTTISH CUP 2001-02

1st Round
Livingston FC Bye

2nd Round
Livingston FC Bye

3rd Round
Albion Rovers 1 Livingston FC 4

4th Round
Aberdeen 2 Livingston FC 0

SCOTTISH CUP 2002-03

3rd Round
Livingston FC 1 Dunfermline Athletic 1
Dunfermline FC 2 Livingston FC 0

SCOTTISH CUP 2003-04

3rd Round
Livingston FC 1 Montrose 0

4th Round
Spartans 0 Livingston FC 4

5th Round
Aberdeen 1 Livingston FC 1
Livingston FC 1 Aberdeen 0

Semi-finals
Livingston FC 1 Celtic 3

SCOTTISH CUP 2004-05

3rd Round
Livingston FC 2   Morton 1

4th Round
Alloa Athletic 0   Livingston FC 1

5th Round
Heart of Midlothian 2   Livingston FC 1

SCOTTISH CUP 2005-06

3rd Round
Alloa Athletic 1   Livingston FC 1
Livingston FC 1   Alloa Athletic 2

SCOTTISH CUP 2006-07

3rd Round
Hamilton Academicals 2   Livingston FC 4

4th Round
Livingston FC 1   Celtic 4

SCOTTISH CUP 2007-08

1st Round
Newton Stewart 0   Linlithgow Rose 6

2nd Round
Linlithgow Rose 4   Spartans 1

3rd Round
Linlithgow Rose 1   Dalbeattie Star 0
Livingston FC 4   Alloa Athletic 0

4th Round
Queen of the South 4 Linlithgow Rose 0
Livingston FC 2 Cowdenbeath 0

5th Round
Livingston FC 0 Partick Thistle 0
Partick Thistle 1 Livingston FC 1
(Partick Thistle win 5-4 on Penalties)

SCOTTISH CUP 2008-09

1st Round
Lochee United 3 Bathgate Thistle 1

3rd Round
East Stirlingshire 2 Livingston FC 1

SCOTTISH CUP 2009-10

2nd Round
Queens Park 1 Livingston FC 3

3rd Round
Clyde 1 Livingston FC 1
Livingston FC 7 Clyde 1

4th Round
Livingston FC 0 Dundee 1

SCOTTISH CUP 2010-11

1st Round
Beith 2 Linlithgow Rose 0
Selkirk 1 Bo'ness United 6

2nd Round
Bo'ness United 2 Queens Park 1

3rd Round
Bo'ness United 0   Buckie Thistle 2
Elgin City 2 Livingston FC 1

SCOTTISH CUP 2011- 12

1st Round
Fort William 0 Bo'ness United 4

2nd Round
Bo'ness United 2   Whitehill Welfare 1

3rd Round
Irvine Meadow 0 Livingston 6
Bo'ness United 0 Cowdenbeath 3

4th Round
Livingston 1 Ayr United 2

SCOTTISH CUP 2012-13

1st Round
Livingston 0 Dundee 2

SCOTTISH CUP 2013-14

1st Round
Linlithgow Rose 2 Nairn County 0

2nd Round
Devronvale 2 Linlithgow Rose 2
Linlithgow Rose 1 Devronvale 3

4th Round
St Johnstone 2 Livingston 0

SCOTTISH CUP 2014-15

1st Round
Selkirk 0 Bo'ness United 4
Fraserburgh 0 Linlithgow Rose 0
Linlithgow Rose 2 Fraserburgh 1

2nd Round
Linlithgow Rose 5 Dalbeattie Star 1
Bo'ness United 7 Culter 1

3rd Round
Linlithgow Rose 0 Raith Rovers 2
Elgin City 4 Bo'ness United 4
Bo'ness United 5 Elgin City 4
Annan Athletic 3 Livingston FC 2

4th Round
Bo'ness United 0 Arbroath FC 5

SCOTTISH CONSOLATION CUP 1907-08 Season

1st Round
Berwick Rangers 3 West Calder Swifts 3
West Calder Swifts 5 Berwick Rangers 1
Broxburn FC 3 East Stirlingshire 3
East Stirlingshire 3 Broxburn FC 1
Broxburn Shamrock 0 Bathgate FC 6
West Lothian Albion 4 Stenhousemuir 1
Clachmannan 0 Broxburn Athletic 1

2nd Round
St Cuthberts Wanderers O Bathgate FC W
West Calder Swifts 3 Broxburn Athletic 3
Broxburn Athletic 0 West Calder Swifts 0
West Calder Swifts 0 Broxburn Athletic 3
West Lothian Albion 0 Leith Athletic 3

3rd Round
Bathgate FC   1   East Stirlingshire   2
Broxburn Athletic   Bye

4th Round
Dumbarton   2   Broxburn Athletic   1   (Game Stopped)
Dumbarton   6   Broxburn Athletic   0

Season 1908-09

1st Round
Broxburn Athletic   4   West Lothian Albion   2
St Bernards   O   Bo'ness FC   W
Uphall FC   O   Bathgate FC   W

2nd Round
Kirkcaldy United   0   Broxburn Athletic   2

East Fife   1   Bathgate FC   0
Lochgelly United   0   Bo'ness FC   0
Bo'ness FC   0   Lochgelly United   1

3rd Round
Broxburn Athletic   Bye

4th Round
Broxburn Athletic   3   Lochgelly United   0

5th Round
Arbroath   2   Broxburn Athletic   1

Season 1909-10

1st Round
Broxburn FC   3   West Calder Swifts   1
Broxburn Athletic   3   Broxburn Shamrock   0
St Bernards   3   West Lothian Albion   0

2nd Round
Broxburn Athletic   1   Broxburn FC   1
Broxburn FC   4   Broxburn Athletic   1

3rd Round
Broxburn FC   Bye

4th Round
East Stirlingshire   1   Broxburn FC   1
Broxburn FC   1   East Stirlingshire   1
East Stirlingshire   3   Broxburn FC   1

Season   1910-11

1st Round
Armadale FC   2   Bathgate FC   1
West Calder Swifts   4   Broxburn Athletic   1
West Lothian Albion   2   Broxburn Shamrock   2
Broxburn Shamrock   0   West Lothian Albion   0
West Lothian Albion   0   Broxburn Shamrock   2
Broxburn FC   Bye

2nd Round
Broxburn Shamrock   0   Berwick Rangers   1
Duns   1   Broxburn FC   2
Peebles Rovers   5   West Calder Swifts   3
Coldstream   0   Armadale FC   0
Armadale FC   8   Coldstream   1

3rd Round
Broxburn FC   1   Armadale FC   0

4th Round
Broxburn FC   2   Clachmannan   1

5th Round
Forres Mechanics   3   Broxburn FC   2

1911-12 Season

1st Round
Broxburn FC   1   Bo'ness FC   1
Bo'ness FC   0   Broxburn FC   0
Broxburn FC   3   Bo'ness FC   0
West Calder Swifts 0   Bathgate FC   3
West Lothian Albion   0   St Bernards   5
Broxburn Shamrock   Bye

2nd Round
Broxburn Shamrock   2   Gala Fairydean   1
St Bernards   2   Broxburn FC   1
Bathgate FC   4   Coldstream   0

3rd Round
St Bernards   8   Broxburn Shamrock   0
Bathgate FC   Bye

4th Round
St Curthberts Wanderers 1   Bathgate FC   5

5th Round
Johnstone   2   Bathgate FC   1

1912-13 Season

1st Round
Armadale FC   2   Leith Amateurs 1
Bathgate FC   1   Broxburn Shamrock   1
Broxburn Shamrock 2   Bathgate FC   3
Bo'ness FC   W   Leith Athletic O

2nd Round
Armadale FC   3   Bo'ness FC   0
Bathgate FC   4   Vale of Leithen 1

208

3rd Round
Bathgate FC   4   Mussleburgh   0
Armadale FC   Bye

4th Round
Beith   1   Bathgate FC   0
Renton   1   Armadale FC   1
Armadale FC   2   Renton   0

5th Round
Armadale FC   2   Beith   3

1913-14 Season

1st Round
Broxburn Shamrock   2   Leith Amateurs   3
Armadale FC   2   Bathgate FC   3
St Bernards   2   Bo'ness FC   0

2nd Round
St Bernards   2   Bathgate FC   0

Worn by
100,000
Players

"Manfield-Hotspur"

22/6

"MANFIELD-HOTSPUR" is more imitated than any Football Boot made.
Thus even competitors bear witness to its supremacy and superior points.
Premier Clubs own its supremacy by their continuous appearance, among
other famous and familiar names, on the roll of "MANFIELD-HOTSPUR"
wearers.

In half-sizes and four widths. Relative prices for boys sizes.

Order early the genuine boot from a Manfield's branch or agency direct,
and avoid the disappointment of getting, "only a substitute."

Manfield
& SONS LTD

Authorised Agent :—

W. L. MORRISON, 211 HIGH STREET —— LINLITHGOW

CATALOGUE POST FREE

DECHMONT FORKLIFT TRUCKS

Mitsubishi & Hamech Specialists

Service, Sales, Hire & Repair of all types of Forklift Trucks.
Service, Sales & Repair to Pallet Trucks.

Dechmont Forklift Trucks Ltd
13 Brocks Way
East Mains Industrial Estate
Broxburn
West Lothian
H52 5NB
Telephone: 01506 859 599

E-mail: info@dechmontforklifttrucks.co.uk

MOT'S SERVICING

MOT'S REPAIRS

37 Livery Street, Bathgate, EH48 4HR
Tel: 01506 630 694

Testing Vehicles for over 20 years, and offer repairs while you wait. We have a comfortable and clean waiting area, with friendly and approachable staff you can talk too.

We have a modern workshop with top of the range equipment, Air-Conditioning, Trained Technicians, Snap-On Diagnostics, and offer full service report with all services.

All work will be priced and agreed with the customer before work is carried out.

Opening Times :-
Mon-Fri :- 8.30am to 5.00pm
Sat :- 8.30am to 12.30pm

Servicing
We offer a wide range of servicing options for most makes and models. Please contact us for pricing and further information.

Tyres
Contact us to check stock levels for your tyre replacement. We are the country's main dealer of Primewell Tyres, quality tyres at a low cost price.

Exhausts
We stock exhausts for most vehicle types, please contact us for prices and availability of stock.

www.aceexhaustsandtyres.co.uk

PUBLISHED BY GUS MARTIN

Printed by Airdrie Print Services